Corporate Acquisitions and Mergers in Switzerland

Corporate Acquisitions and Mergers in Switzerland

Third Edition

Elisa Aliotta
Reto Arpagaus
Michael Barrot
Claudio Bazzi
Adrian Bieri
Kurt Blickenstorfer
Nicola Corvi
Ion Eglin
Tobias Herren
Barbara Jecklin
Cédric Jenoure
Florian S. Jörg
Harald Maag
Martin Moser
Daniel Mosimann
Thomas Peter
Pascal Rüedi
Thomas Schönenberger
Christian Wind
Sascha Wohlgemuth

Bratschi Ltd.

This book was originally published as a chapter in Corporate Acquisitions and Mergers.

General Editor: Peter Begg

Wolters Kluwer

Published by:
Kluwer Law International B.V.
PO Box 316
2400 AH Alphen aan den Rijn
The Netherlands
E-mail: lrs-sales@wolterskluwer.com
Website: www.wolterskluwer.com/en/solutions/kluwerlawinternational

Sold and distributed by:
Wolters Kluwer Legal & Regulatory U.S.
7201 McKinney Circle
Frederick, MD 21704
United States of America
E-mail: customer.service@wolterskluwer.com

ISBN 978-94-035-4364-2

e-Book: ISBN 978-94-035-4994-1
web-PDF: ISBN 978-94-035-4335-2

Contents

Bratschi Ltd.

Bratschi Ltd. is one of Switzerland's leading and rapidly growing law firms with over one hundred lawyers. It is a full-service law firm offering clients a broad range of first-class legal and counselling services with a focus on M&A transactions, corporate law in general, contracts, tax law as well as litigation and arbitration.

Experienced attorneys of Bratschi Ltd. advise and represent national and international enterprises, in particular, medium-sized companies as well as private individuals and the public sector with great commitment. In each case, the best team of lawyers for the clients' needs is set in place and a personal and long-term client relationship is cultivated. Bratschi Ltd. provides its clients with one-stop assistance from its six major business centres in Switzerland (listed below). It also has a notarial service with branches in Basel, St. Gallen and Zug, where certifications and authentications are offered.

Zurich	**Basel**	**Bern**
Bratschi Ltd. Bahnhofstrasse 70 P.O. Box CH-8021 Zurich Tel.: +41 58 258 10 00 Fax: +41 58 258 10 99	Bratschi Ltd. Lange Gasse 15 P.O. Box CH-4002 Basel Tel.: +41 58 258 19 00 Fax: +41 58 258 19 99	Bratschi Ltd. Bollwerk 15 P.O. Box CH-3001 Bern Tel.: +41 58 258 16 00 Fax: +41 58 258 16 99
Lausanne	**St. Gallen**	**Zug**
Bratschi Ltd. Avenue Mon-Repos 14 P.O. Box 5507 CH-1002 Lausanne Tel.: +41 58 258 17 00 Fax: +41 58 258 17 99	Bratschi Ltd. Vadianstrasse 44 P.O. Box 262 CH-9001 St.Gallen Tel.: +41 58 258 14 00 Fax: +41 58 258 14 99	Bratschi Ltd. Gubelstrasse 11 CH-6300 Zug Tel.: +41 58 258 18 00 Fax: +41 58 258 18 99

Geneva		
Bratschi AG Rue du Général-Dufour 20 P.O. Box CH-1211 Genève Tel.: +41 58 258 13 00 Fax: +41 58 258 17 99		

Authors

The following authors have contributed to this handbook with their topics:

Elisa Aliotta	Future developments
Reto Arpagaus	Shareholder approval rights, directors' duties, form of consideration, dividends, acquisition of own shares, corporate veil and the piercing thereof, insolvency, choice of law and jurisdiction or arbitration
Michael Barrot	Nature of Swiss tax regime, liability for tax/tax consolidation, group relief of gains and losses, withholding taxes
Claudio Bazzi	Local economic, political and cultural aspects
Adrian Bieri	Intellectual property and other relevant laws
Kurt Blickenstorfer	Dispute resolution and enforcement (coordination of all contributions)
Nicola Corvi	Tax considerations arising from M&A transactions, structuring of investment, debt financing, thin capitalisation, transfer pricing, withholding taxes
Ion Eglin	Business vehicles
Tobias Herren	Employment considerations
Barbara Jecklin	Financial assistance, security interests
Cédric Jenoure	Accounting treatment, withholding taxes
Florian S. Jörg	Relevant regulatory authorities, no restrictions on foreign investments

Harald Maag	Laws and regulations for combining and dividing companies
Martin Moser	Laws affecting M&A
Daniel Mosi-mann	Business vehicles
Thomas Peter	Due diligence
Pascal Rüedi	Specific rules on public takeovers, banking, insurance and financial services
Thomas Schönenberger	Restrictions on foreign directors or managers, no permit to trade for a foreign-owned company, in general
Christian Wind	Merger controls, antitrust and competition issues
Sascha Wohlge-muth	Accounting treatment, withholding taxes

List of Abbreviations

AIG	Swiss Aliens and Integration Act
AG	Aktiengesellschaft, Ltd
AFMP	Agreement on the Free Movement of Persons Concluded Between Switzerland and the European Union
AHV	Swiss Old Age and Survivors' Insurance
AHVG	Swiss Act on Old Age and Survivors' Insurance
AMLA	Swiss Anti-Money Laundering Act
Anti-Cartels Act	Swiss Federal Act on Cartels and Other Restraints of Competition
approx.	Approximately
Banking Act	Swiss Act on Banks and Savings Banks
BEPS	Base Erosion and Profit Shifting Project of the OECD
BIS	Bank for International Settlements
CbCR	Country-by-Country Reporting Obligations
CC	Swiss Civil Code
CEO	Chief Executive Officer
CFC	Controlled Foreign Corporation Rules
cf.	Compare
CHF	Swiss Francs
CO	Swiss Code of Obligations
DEBA	Swiss Debt Enforcement and Bankruptcy Act
DETEC	Swiss Federal Department of Environment, Transport, Energy and Communications
EBIT	Earnings Before Interest and Taxes
EC	European Community
EFTA	European Free Trade Association

EMEA	Europe, Middle-East & Africa
ETH	Swiss Federal Institute of Technology
et seq.	and the following
EU	European Union
FAC	Swiss Federal Administrative Court
FinIA	Swiss Federal Act on Financial Institutions
FINMA	Swiss Financial Market Supervisory Authority
FinSA	Swiss Federal Act on Financial Services
FMIA	Swiss Financial Market Infrastructure Act
FTA	Swiss Federal Tax Administration
G20	Group of Twenty
GDP	Gross Domestic Product
GmbH	Gesellschaft mit beschränkter Haftung, LLC
HH Index	Herfindahl-Hirschman Index
ICC	International Chamber of Commerce
IMF	International Monetary Fund
IP	Intellectual Property
KLG	Kollektivgesellschaft, General Partnership
KMAG	Kommanditaktiengesellschaft, Partnership Limited by Shares
Lex Koller	Swiss Federal Act on Acquisition of Real Property by Foreigners
LLC	Limited Liability Company
Ltd	Company Limited by Shares
LugConv	Lugano Convention on Jurisdiction and the Recognition and Enforcement of Judgments in Civil and Commercial Matters

Merger Act	Swiss Federal Act on Mergers, Demergers, Transformations and Transfer of Assets
Merger Control Ordinance	Swiss Ordinance on the Control of Concentrations of Undertakings
M&A	Mergers and Acquisitions
New York Convention	Convention on the Recognition and Enforcement of Foreign Arbitral Awards Concluded in New York in 1958
OECD	Organisation for Economic Co-operation and Development
PC	Swiss Penal Code
PE	Permanent Establishment
PILA	Swiss Federal Act on Private International Law
PPA	Purchase Price Allocation
SA	Société Anonyme, Ltd
Sarl	Société à Responsabilité Limitée, LLC
SCMA	Société en Commandite par Actions, Partnership Limited by Shares
SCCP	Swiss Code of Civil Procedure
SCC	Swiss Competition Commission
SECA	Swiss Private Equity & Corporate Finance Association
SECO	Swiss State Secretariat for Economic Affairs
SEM	Swiss Secretariat for Migration
SESTA	Swiss Federal Act on Stock Exchanges and Securities Trading
SFSC	Swiss Federal Supreme Court
SICAF	Société d'Investissement à Capital Fixe, Investment Company with Fixed Capital
SICAV	Société d'Investissement à Capital Variable, Investment Company with Variable Capital
SME	Small- and Medium-Sized Enterprises

SNC	Société en Nom Collectif, General Partnership
TOB	Swiss Takeover Board
UK-BA	United Kingdom Bribery Act
UNCITRAL	United Nations Commission on International Trade Law
UNCTAD	United Nations Conference on Trade and Development
USD	United States Dollar
US-FCPA	United States Foreign Corrupt Practices Act
VAT	Value Added Tax
WHT	Withholding Tax
WTO	World Trade Organization

1 LOCAL ECONOMIC, POLITICAL AND CULTURAL ASPECTS

(by Claudio Bazzi)

1.1 General Comments on the Country Profile

1.1.1 European Country, Global Player

[01] Switzerland lies at the heart of Europe. It is not a member of the European Union (EU), but merely part of the European single market. Being politically independent, Switzerland has close economic and cultural ties with the countries of the EU. Beyond that, it is a very *open country integrated into the global economy* with a high rate of innovation and productivity. Although Switzerland accounts for only 0.1% of both the world's surface area and population, it continuously ranks among the 20 largest national economies in the world in terms of gross domestic product (GDP) and consequently – from a purely economic point of view – is a G20 country. This, coupled with a number of favourable location factors, makes it an extremely attractive market for national and international M&A activities.

1.1.2 Switzerland in a Nutshell

Facts and Figures

[02] Switzerland has a population of about 8.6 million with a relatively stable growth rate of 1% in recent years, mainly due to external immigration. Switzerland is a federal state with twenty-six Member States, which are called cantons. The political system is characterised by *federalism* (strong autonomy of the cantons), *subsidiarity* (task solution at the lowest possible hierarchical level) and *inclusivity* (direct participation of the people in popular initiatives and referendums).

[03] The country is divided into different cultural areas with four official national languages – *German, French, Italian and Romansh*. German accounts for almost two-thirds and French for about a quarter of the languages spoken. The most common foreign language in Switzerland nowadays is English, driven by the immigration of qualified foreign specialists. Although communication with the authorities must take place in one of the national languages (depending on the entity concerned), some cantons accommodate this autonomous reality by publishing official information and documents in English.

Natural Resources

[04] Switzerland is a country which is relatively poor in resources. As a result, it strived at an early stage to compensate for its comparative competitive disadvantages through increased efforts in the field of education and innovation. Thanks to its numerous Alpine springs, Switzerland is regarded as the *'moated castle of Europe'*.

In view of the irreplaceability and increasing scarcity of water, this raw material i likely to gain in importance in the future and become another strategic asset fo Switzerland.

Currency

[05] Switzerland's currency is the Swiss franc, which has enjoyed *exceptional stabilit* over the past decades. In recent years marked by global economic and state crise the COVID-19 pandemic and the Russian aggression against Ukraine, the Swis franc has increasingly served as a safe-haven currency for foreign investors, whic is why there has been considerable upward pressure. The Swiss National Bank i attempting to counter this pressure by intervening in the foreign exchange marke without being able to prevent the Swiss franc from being overvalued against th euro and US dollar. However, the Swiss economy, which is heavily dependent o external trade, has adapted relatively well to this situation and is recording soli growth rates.

Labour Market

[06] Even following the COVID-19 pandemic Switzerland has a robust labour mar ket with low unemployment rates, currently around 2.5% (considered as *full emplo ment*). The median wage in Switzerland is around CHF6 500 per month (2018 which is one of the highest in the world. Due to the early focus on education an innovation, three-quarters of GDP is nowadays generated in the service secto Accordingly, Switzerland – together with its excellent universities such as Swiss Fed eral Institute of Technology (ETH) and its dual education system consisting c apprenticeship and vocational school – is well equipped to master transformatio into a digital economy.

Physical Infrastructure

[07] Based on very sound public finances, the physical infrastructure for both pri vate and public transport is *well developed* in Switzerland. Distances, which are sho anyway due to the small size of the country can be overcome quickly and comfor ably: journeys on the east-west axis between Zurich and Geneva take approx. thre hours by car or train, and on the north-south axis between Zurich and Lugano onl two hours by car or train.

1.2 Government and Political System

1.2.1 General Political Environment

[08] Politically, Switzerland has been very stable for decades. This stability i ensured not least by the *tradition of direct democracy*, which allows the Swiss people t take corrective action and ensures that there is no excessive concentration of powe among individuals or political parties. Accordingly, there is great continuity an reliability with regard to the political, economic and legal framework in Switzerland.

1.2.2 Attractiveness for Entrepreneurs and Investors

[09] Switzerland is organised as an *open and liberal market economy*. Swiss economic policy, therefore, aims to regulate markets only in case of market failure and if the cost of government intervention is lower compared to non-action. This economic policy backdrop – together with a highly educated and innovative workforce – forms an excellent environment for entrepreneurs. Switzerland is regularly well-placed in international entrepreneur rankings.

[10] Likewise, it is an attractive market for both domestic and foreign investors. Besides the Lex Koller (*see* paragraph [118]), there are *no protectionist barriers* in place for foreign investors preventing them from investing in Switzerland.

1.2.3 Interlinking with Global Financial System

[11] As an open and liberal market economy with a *long tradition in international banking*, Switzerland is closely integrated into the global financial market architecture, both at the private and the institutional levels. Some of the world's leading universal banks, such as UBS and Credit Suisse, are headquartered in Switzerland.

[12] At the political level, Switzerland is an *active member* of major international financial and trade *organisations* such as the World Trade Organization (WTO), European Free Trade Association (EFTA), Organisation for Economic Co-operation and Development (OECD), International Monetary Fund (IMF) and World Bank. In addition, Switzerland is associated with the G20 Finance Track and thus participates in the G20 Finance Ministers' meetings and various working group meetings in the field of international financial market policy. It is also the host state of the Bank for International Settlements (BIS).

1.3 Legal System

1.3.1 Legal Tradition

[13] Switzerland stands in the continental European legal tradition. The basis for the application of the law is provided by the laws and ordinances enacted at the various state levels (confederation, cantons, municipalities), in each case depending on the powers conferred by the constitution. Compared to its European neighbours, *private autonomy* is weighted more strongly in Switzerland. For example, flexibility in contractual arrangements, such as in the area of labour law, is considerably higher than in other European countries.

1.3.2 Law Enforcement

[14] Institutions and laws have a high level of acceptance among the Swiss pop lation due to the latter's direct democratic say. Hence great importance is attache to law enforcement at all levels and in all areas of law. Private law enforcement relatively easy to obtain in Switzerland. Access to courts is guaranteed everywhe and proceedings are generally *efficient and expeditious*. Zurich as Switzerland's bus ness centre features a Commercial Court specialising in commercial dispute which has the specialist knowledge required for the assessment of M&A cases. Fu thermore, Switzerland is also an international hub for arbitration with excelle legal practitioners. This provides international investors with the valid option agreeing on the jurisdiction of an arbitral tribunal for the enforcement of ar claims arising in the context of M&A transactions.

1.4 Current Economic Aspects

1.4.1 Actual and Projected Growth Rates

[15] After the worldwide economic slump in 2020 caused by the COVID-19 pa demic which also extended to Switzerland, as early as mid-2021 the Swiss econ my's growth rates reached pre-crisis levels. The Federal Government's expe group is currently forecasting GDP growth of around 3% for 2022 and around 2 for 2023 as the global economy is expected to normalise. However, further setbac in fighting the COVID-19 pandemic slowing down economic recovery cannot b fully ruled out. Other economic risks include the capacity bottlenecks and disru tions in global supply chains as well as the recent increases in inflation which mig translate into price pressure and rising long-term interest rates. Finally, the Russia invasion of Ukraine followed by severe sanctions from Western countries will like have a negative impact on economic growth.

1.4.2 M&A Trends

[16] After the M&A activity crashed globally in 2020 because of the COVID-1 pandemic, in 2021 Switzerland's M&A market regained confidence and returne to record levels. Forecasts by experts assume that the M&A market in Switzerlan will remain very robust in 2022 due to the accelerated recovery of the economy. O the other hand, recent geopolitical challenges, particularly the war in Ukrain might slow down M&A activity both internationally and domestically.

[17] Switzerland, with its high political and economic stability and resilience, is tr ditionally regarded as a safe haven in times of increased investment risks. It therefore expected that *Switzerland and its well-positioned companies will remain attra tive* acquisition targets (despite the ongoing war in Ukraine). This will continue be promoted by influential Swiss investment banks, contributing to matchmakin between sellers and acquirers.

1.5 Main Industries

1.5.1 Key Sectors

[18] The service sector accounts for approximately 75% of GDP whereas industry contributes approximately 25% to GDP (agriculture is worth less than 1%). Key sectors include the *financial industry, commodities, high-tech, micro-technology, biotechnology as well as chemicals and pharmaceuticals*. Apart from some well-known publicly listed multinational enterprises such as Nestlé, Novartis, Glencore or UBS, Switzerland is home to more than 600 000 private businesses. Ninety-nine per cent of all businesses are small- and medium-sized enterprises (SMEs) employing approximately 65% of the workforce.

1.5.2 Role of the State in the Economy

[19] *Switzerland largely abstains from industrial policy* and does not foster strategic sectors or firms. Rather, economic policy focuses on framework conditions such as high levels of education, flexibility of the labour market, lean bureaucratic processes and a well-developed infrastructure. Markets are generally left to private enterprises only. However, the state holds certain monopolies and acts as the sole or major shareholder of private companies in certain areas deemed relevant to basic public services or strategic infrastructure, especially in public transport, postal services, telecommunications and energy supply.

1.5.3 Protectionist Measures vis-à-vis Foreign Investors

[20] By nature, state-owned companies are excluded from private investments, be it domestic or foreign. Besides that, acquisition of real estate property and of shares in companies that own *real estate is regulated* by the Lex Koller (*see* paragraph [118]). If real estate held by a Swiss target company is used for business purposes only, authorisation does not have to be obtained from the competent cantonal authority. However, if the assets of a target company include residential real estate or significant land reserves, the authorisation requirement might be triggered. Where there is doubt, it is advisable to seek official confirmation from the competent cantonal authority that no approval is needed. This can significantly slow down the transaction process as it normally takes approximately two months to obtain such confirmation. Finally, general clearance processes such as merger control or sector-specific authorisation requirements must be observed (*see* paragraphs [90] et seq.).

1.5.4 Investor Characteristics

[21] Traditionally, the Swiss M&A market is *equally dominated by strategic and financial buyers*. The persistently favourable interest rate environment provides a lot of capital for M&A activities. Private equity investors and venture capitalists continue to benefit from this as they typically operate with high debt ratios. On the other hand, many strategic investors also have full pockets at their disposal for acqui tions of well-positioned Swiss companies.

1.6 Cultural Aspects

[22] There is no doubt that Switzerland can be considered one of the most attra tive places to do business worldwide. Switzerland benefits from a variety of favou able location factors such as security, stable and efficient institutions, independent and fair judiciary, well-developed infrastructure, sound pub finances (even after unprecedented government interventions in response to t COVID-19 pandemic), monetary stability, an educated workforce, a flexible labo market as well as openness to foreign trade and investment. Cost levels in Switze land are generally elevated. However, this must be seen against the backgrou that wages adjusted for purchasing power are among the highest in the world. Sw zerland as a member of many of the standard-setting international organisatio *lives up fully to Western business patterns*, and no specific issues have to be noted. Als levels of business ethics and integrity are among the highest with no room at all f corrupt practices.

2 THE REGULATORY FRAMEWORK

2.1 Business Vehicles

(by Ion Eglin, Daniel Mosimann)

2.1.1 Overview of Corporate Forms and Company Types

[23] In Switzerland, a distinction is made between sole proprietorships and co panies. According to Swiss company law, a further distinction is made between t following types of companies:

Capital companies: Company limited by shares, limited liability compa (LLC), partnership limited by shares and investment companies with varial capital or fixed capital.

Partnerships: Simple partnership, general partnership, limited partnership a limited partnership for collective investment schemes.

Cooperative companies In this contribution, the focus falls on companies, esp cially on the most common types of companies, such as the company limited shares and the LLC.

2.1.2 Capital Companies

Company Limited by Shares [Ltd] (Aktiengesellschaft [AG], Société Anonyme [SA])

[24] A company limited by shares may be established by one or more natural persons or legal entities or other commercial enterprises and is subject to authentication and notarisation by a notary public. Only the company assets are liable for the liabilities of an Ltd; thus, in the event of bankruptcy, the shareholders can lose most of their share capital. The *share capital* of the Ltd must be at least *CHF100 000*. As a minimum, 20% of the share capital, but always at least CHF50 000 must be paid in. The capital does not necessarily have to be paid in cash. It can also be contributed in the form of existing assets (e.g., real estate, machines, intellectual property (IP), cryptocurrencies) or offsetting of claims, both forms called contribution in kind (which requires some additional documentation). The share capital can be later increased or decreased, to the minimum of CHF100 000, but any change in the share capital must be publicly notarised and registered with the Commercial Register.

[25] An Ltd can only be founded with *registered shares*. Bearer shares are only permissible as an exception if specific requirements are met. Shares must have a nominal value of at least 1 cent per share. It is possible to issue voting shares, participation certificates, dividend right certificates and preference shares. *Shareholders* remain anonymous and are not entered in the Commercial Register. However, the company must keep a *non-public register* of all shareholders (name and address), plus the beneficial owners (name and address) of shareholders who control capital or voting rights in excess of 25%. Apart from paying in the share capital, a shareholder has no other statutory obligations. Additional compulsory obligations, may, however, be introduced by the conclusion of a shareholders' agreement. On the other hand, a shareholder has certain rights, such as the right to participate in the general meeting, minimum voting rights, the right to take action (in case of a violation of their rights) and the right to receive information. Furthermore, shareholders are protected by qualified *decision quorums* for important decisions of the general meeting. Shares can be transferred by way of written assignment. Where the articles of association provide that the shares have restricted transferability, transfer is subject to approval by the board of directors. Due to the external anonymity of the shareholders, however, there is no obligation to register any changes with the Commercial Register.

[26] The *corporate bodies* of the Ltd are the general meeting of shareholders as the supreme governing body, the board of directors as the executive body and the auditors, if elected and not opted out, as the (accounting) controlling body. The board of directors is elected by the general meeting of shareholders and consists of one or more members. There are no requirements regarding nationality or domicile for directors, but at least one director or manager with sole signing authority or two directors or managers with dual signing authority must be domiciled in Switzerland.

[27] The *board of directors* may fully or partially delegate the management of th company to individual members or third parties, who do not have to be sharehold ers, by establishing organisational regulations. Typically, transferable duties of th board of directors are delegated to a single director (delegate of the board of direc tors) or an executive board (Chief Executive Officer (CEO) and members). Th members of the board of directors (and any managers or other authorised signato ries) with *signing authority* are listed in the Commercial Register and all change must be filed with the Commercial Register. Within the scope of their authority t sign, the registered directors or managers are authorised to perform all legal act on behalf of the company and to provide all necessary signatures which the pur pose of the company may entail. An additional, explicit power of attorney is nc required to represent the company and any restrictions of an (internal) power c attorney cannot be invoked against a third party acting in good faith.

[28] Companies have either an ordinary *audit*, a limited audit or they can waive th audit, depending on the following conditions: listed companies and companie that exceed two of the following three thresholds in two successive financial years balance sheet total of CHF20 m, revenue of CHF40 m, and 250 full-time position on annual average. If these requirements are not met and if shareholders repre senting a total share capital of 10% do not request an *ordinary audit* (and if th articles of association do not prescribe such ordinary audit), then the company ma have a so-called limited audit only. With the consent of all shareholders, even thi limited audit can be waived if the company has no more than ten full-time employ ees on annual average (so-called opting out of the audit).

[29] Companies are obliged to draw up and present *accounts*. The general meetin of shareholders has the non-transferable power to approve the annual account and pass resolutions on the allocation of the disposable profit, and, in particular, t determine the dividend and shares of profits paid to board members.

[30] In view of compliance, it must be noted that all Swiss companies are obliged t ensure that their business activity is in *compliance* with all the legal requirement imposed by Swiss law, in particular, the provisions relating to corporate gover nance, for example in the Swiss Code of Obligations (CO), Merger Act, Swiss Audi Supervision Act and Swiss Penal Code (PC).

[31] Despite the high minimum capital, the Ltd is still the *most common company typ* for foreign investors, mainly due to the external anonymity of the shareholders an simple share transferability.

Limited Liability Company [LLC] (Gesellschaft mit beschränkter Haftung [GmbH], société responsabilité limitée [sarl])

[32] An LLC can be established by one or more natural persons or legal entities o other commercial enterprises. The *nominal capital* must be at least *CHF20 000* an the nominal value of the capital contribution (quotas) must be at least CHF100. I contrast to the Ltd, the capital amount must be fully paid in. All other aspects of th formation process correspond to the Ltd (notarisation required for incorporatior contributions in kind are possible). In contrast to the Ltd, the owners of the capita must be entered in the Commercial Register. As a result, transfers of shares require a bit more paperwork and are *visible to the public* in the Commercial Register.

[33] Another difference to the Ltd is the duty of loyalty: as a matter of principle, the *partners* of an LLC are obliged to act loyal to the company and to safeguard the interests of the company. The articles of association can further stipulate a non-competition provision and subsequent contributions or ancillary duties which are then automatically applicable and valid for all partners – whereas every shareholder of an Ltd would have to agree and execute a separate contract, the shareholders' agreement.

[34] The *corporate bodies* of the LLC are the general meeting of partners as the supreme governing body, the management board as the executive body and the auditors, if any, as the (accounting) controlling body. To the extent that nothing to the contrary is stipulated in the articles of association, each member of the management board is entitled to represent the company. At least one member of the management board must be authorised to represent the company, whereby at least one person with sole signing authority or two persons with dual signing authority must be domiciled in Switzerland.

[35] With regard to auditing, accounting obligations and compliance, reference can be made in full to the comments on the company limited by shares (cf. paragraphs [28] et seq.).

[36] The LLC is particularly suitable for business with only a *few partners* and not only their financial investment but also their *personal involvement*. The downside, however, is the lack of anonymity of the partners and their duties.

Partnership Limited by Shares (Kommanditaktiengesellschaft [KMAG], société en commandite par actions [SCMA])

[37] A partnership limited by shares is a partnership with a capital divided into shares and with *one or more partners who have unlimited joint and several liability* to its creditors in the same manner as partners in a general partnership. The partners with unlimited liability constitute the directors of the SCMA. They are responsible for business management and representation and must be named in the articles of association.

Investment Company with Variable Capital (Investmentgesellschaft mit variablem Kapital, société d'investissement à capital variable [SICAV])

[38] The investment company *with variable capital* is a business tool which is largely based on the rules of the Ltd and has the sole *purpose of collective capital investment*. The capital is not determined in advance. Company shareholders of investment companies with variable capital that are self-managed must provide a minimum investment of CHF500 000 at the time of formation, and in the case of external management CHF250 000 at the time of formation. Formation and operation are subject to *supervision by Swiss Financial Market Supervisory Authority (FINMA)*. The

establishment and obtaining of the relevant permits mean that this company for
is only suitable for foreign companies with appropriate qualifications.

Investment Company with Fixed Capital (Investmentgesellschaft mit fixem Kapital, socié d'investissement à capital fixe [SICAF])

[39] The investment company *with fixed capital* is a company limited by shares pu suant to the CO which is not listed on a Swiss stock exchange and has the sole *pu pose of the investment of collective capital*. The shareholders do not have to be qualifie investors pursuant to the Collective Investment Schemes Act. In contrast to th Ltd, no voting shares, participation certificates, dividend right certificates an preference shares may be issued and the appointment of an audit company is ma datory. Formation and operation of the company are also subject to *supervision FINMA*. This company form is also only suitable for foreign companies with appr priate qualifications.

2.1.3 Partnerships

Simple Partnership (Einfache Gesellschaft, société simple)

[40] A simple partnership is the *most basic form of partnership*. It is a contractu (written or oral) relationship where two or more individuals or legal entities agre to combine their efforts or resources in order to achieve a common goal rather tha a legal entity. Generally, the *partners are jointly and severally liable* for company deb with all their own assets. Any partnership that does not fulfil the distinctive criter of any of the other types of partnership codified in the CO is considered a simp partnership. There are *no formal requirements* and the parties involved in a simp partnership may not even be aware that they are partners in a simple partnershi before disputes regarding loss participation or tax consequences arise. All partne have the right to manage the partnership unless the task is entrusted exclusively one or more partners or to third parties by agreement or resolution.

[41] Because of the personal liability, this form of company is not favoured by fo eign investors for business purposes.

General Partnership (Kollektivgesellschaft [KLG], société en nom collectif [SNC])

[42] A general partnership is a partnership between *two or more natural perso* (legal entities are excluded) who jointly operate a trading, manufacturing or oth forms of commercial business under one business name, without limiting their pe sonal liability. Consequently, the *partners are jointly and severally liable* for the debts their business operations with their private assets. Every partner has basically th same rights and duties (e.g., the same voting rights and the same claim to pro and loss). Shares in a general partnership are in principle non-transferable an non-heritable.

[43] The partnership is *not a legal entity* but may acquire rights, assume obligations, sue and be sued. Non-commercial partnerships must be registered in the Commercial Register and are only incorporated upon registration, while commercial partnerships start to exist with the execution of the agreement between the partners. Basically, bona fide third parties may safely assume that every partner has the authority to represent the partnership.

[44] This legal form is particularly suitable for activities that are *strongly linked to the partners* and is often chosen by small companies managed by several persons (e.g., local craft enterprises or restaurants), but it is not very widespread among foreign investors.

Limited Partnership (Kommanditgesellschaft [KMG], Société en commandit [SCM])

[45] A limited partnership is a partnership between two or more persons who jointly operate a business in such a manner that at least one partner is an unlimited partner with unlimited liability and one or more partners have limited liability. The *unlimited partners* must be natural persons, but limited partners can also be legal entities. The unlimited partners are jointly and severally liable with all their assets for all obligations of the partnership, whereas the *limited partners* are only liable to third parties for their contribution, which is registered in the Commercial Register.

[46] In principle, the partnership is managed by the partners with unlimited liability. However, a limited partner conducting business on behalf of the partnership without expressly stating that he is acting as registered attorney or commercial agent is liable to bona fide third parties for all obligations resulting from such business as if he were an unlimited partner.

[47] Like the general partnership, limited partnerships are not considered common business tools for foreign companies.

Limited Partnership for Collective Investment Schemes (Kommanditgesellschaft für kollektive Kapitalanlagen, société en commandite de placements collectifs)

[48] The limited partnership for collective investment schemes is another form of a company for *collective investment schemes*, alongside investment companies with variable capital or fixed capital (cf. paragraphs [38] and [39]). Its purpose is a collective investment and to bring the capital of investors together. Like the 'common' limited partnership, at least one partner bears unlimited liability, whereas the *limited members* are only liable in the amount of their specific contributions.

[49] The *unlimited partner* of a limited partnership for collective investment schemes must be an Ltd and its formation and operation are subject to *supervision by FINMA*. Furthermore, *only qualified investors* may participate in a limited partnership for collective investment schemes. This business tool is neither widespread in Switzerland nor can it be considered common for foreign companies.

2.1.4 Cooperative Company (Genossenschaft, Société Coopérative)

[50] A cooperative is a corporate entity consisting of at *least seven persons or comm-cial enterprises*, joining for the primary purpose of promoting or safeguarding t specific economic interests of the society's members. Cooperatives with a predete mined nominal capital are not permitted.

[51] The cooperative is governed by the *'principle of the open door'*, which means th the cooperative must be open to an unlimited number of members and entry m not be excessively difficult. Every member has one vote (principle of head voic irrespective of their capital share. Although a business purpose can also be follow under the legal form of a cooperative, in most cases cooperatives are established promote certain economic interests of their members (e.g., housing cooperative The cooperative has established itself as a form of company for local enterpris especially in the food retail market, but is not particularly popular among forei companies.

2.2 Laws Affecting M&A

(by Florian S. Jörg, Harald Maag, Martin Moser, Pascal Rüedi, Thomas Schöne berger)

2.2.1 Main Laws and Regulations Involved in M&A Activity

[52] M&A transactions are governed by various statute laws and case law prec dents. However, there is *no statute law that would specifically regulate such transactio* at least as far as privately held Swiss entities are concerned. With regard to laws an or regulations involved in M&A activities, a distinction must be made betwe privately-held entities and companies listed on a stock exchange.

[53] With regard to transactions involving privately held entities, in particular t *general provisions on the sale of goods* as set forth in Articles 184 et seq. CO, app However, to a large extent, these are not mandatory provisions. Moreover, becau the statutory provisions in many respects are not suitable for M&A transactions, t parties typically agree (heavily influenced by the Anglo-American drafting style) transaction agreements on terms they deem appropriate, and they have conside able flexibility under the law.

[54] Mergers of entities, restructurings such as spin-offs or changes from one leg form to another as well as transfers of assets are governed by the *Merger Act*.

[55] In the case of public (i.e., listed) companies, a number of specific laws a regulations apply (*see* paragraphs [58] et seq.) to transactions involving listed co panies).

[56] In addition, many (statutory) laws and regulations now have an impact M&A transactions. Some of these laws and regulations are expressly referred elsewhere. The following areas are just two examples:

(1) Merger control governed by the Anti-Cartels Act (*see* paragraphs [390] et seq).
(2) Acquisition of real property by foreigners governed by the Lex Koller (*see* paragraphs [118] et seq).

Laws and Regulations for Different Types of Company or Different Types of Transaction

[57] As mentioned above, different laws/regulations apply to transactions involving privately held entities from those applicable to listed companies. And, as mentioned above, certain types of transactions (e.g., mergers) are governed in particular by the Merger Act. Otherwise, the rules and regulations are essentially the same.

Main Differences Between Private and Public Deals

[58] *Private deals* are regulated much less strictly than public deals and because of their *contractual freedom*, the parties to a private M&A transaction are to a large extent free to determine the rules that will apply to the transaction. In particular, in private M&A deals the transaction documents do not need to be published and the parties are free to agree on the sale of a majority of the shares without any obligation for the buyer to make an offer to all of the remaining shareholders. In addition, parties to a private deal in general are free to agree on the purchase price per share.

[59] In contrast, *public takeover offers* for listed companies as defined by the Swiss Financial Market Infrastructure Act (FMIA), i.e., companies with their registered office in Switzerland whose equity securities are at least partly listed on a stock exchange in Switzerland or companies with their registered office abroad whose equity securities are at least in part mainly listed in Switzerland, are *governed by the rules of Swiss takeover law*. The FMIA highly regulates public takeover offers (*see* paragraphs [192] et seq.).

Differences Between Friendly and Agreed or Hostile Transactions

[60] A distinction between friendly and hostile transactions has only been made in the area of listed companies. In this area, however, the applicable provisions may very well differ (*see* paragraphs [192] et seq. on transactions involving listed companies).

2.2.2 Laws and Regulations for Combining and Dividing Companies

Overview

[61] In private transactions, businesses are usually acquired by the purchase of either shares or (all or part of) the assets and liabilities. The most common form of acquisition in Switzerland is the *share purchase*, *inter alia* also for tax reasons (*see* paragraph [483]). Businesses can also be combined by a joint-venture agreemen pursuant to which certain assets are transferred to a new company in exchange fo shares. A public offer is the most common way to obtain control of a public com pany. Public offers may be structured as tender offers for cash or as exchange offer for securities or as a combination of both (including mix and match).

[62] Another way of obtaining control of a company, either public or private, is b *statutory merger*. A statutory merger is executed by absorption (one company is dis solved and merged into another) or by combination (two companies are dissolve and merged into a newly formed company). In both cases, the assets and liabilitie of the dissolved companies are transferred by operation of law to the surviving o new company. Shares and cash may be used as consideration. If shareholders ar forced to accept compensation other than shares of the surviving compan (squeeze-out), 90% of all voting securities outstanding need to approve.

[63] As alternatives to a statutory merger, *share-for-share transactions* (so-calle quasi-merger) or the formation of a new company which takes over the assets an liabilities of the two combined companies in exchange for its own shares can b pursued.

[64] In transactions where a company divests part of its assets or liabilities to on or more acquiring entities, the parties may choose to execute the resulting busines combination by way of a statutory *demerger*. In such a case, the assets and liabilitie of the divesting legal entity are transferred by operation of law to the acquirin company, and the shareholders of the divesting legal entity receive shares in th acquiring company as consideration.

[65] Business combinations are, in general, governed by the CO and the Merge Act. Public offers for listed shares are, in addition, subject to Swiss Federal Act o Stock Exchanges and Securities Trading (SESTA). SESTA applies to cash or shar exchange offers addressed publicly to the holders of equity securities of companie whose equity securities are listed on a Swiss exchange.

Acquisition of Shares

[66] In a share purchase, the buyer buys the *shares of the target company* from th shareholders rather than buying the business directly from the target company. A a rule, share purchase agreements provide for detailed and extensive *representation and warranties*, based on the specific risks discovered during the due diligence pro cess, and are tailored to the business being purchased. Swiss law does not provid for a specific legal regime applicable to the sale of a company. Thus, unless the par ties agree to specific representations and warranties, the general provisions of Swis contract law (CO) relating to the sale of personal property apply. The Swis Supreme Court has held that in the case of a share purchase agreement, only th shares are the subject of the sale – and not the business. Therefore, the statutor remedies available to the buyer only cover the share certificates themselves (owner ship, valid issuance, etc.) but not the business, because the business is only pur chased indirectly (*see also* paragraph [373]). It is therefore important for buyers t request specific representations and warranties relating to the business to b acquired, as they cannot rely on the statutory remedies. Representations and warranties should be tailored to the risks of the business to be acquired.

[67] According to Swiss law, the buyer must *examine* the quality of the subject of the purchase as soon as it is customary in accordance with usual business practice (*see* paragraphs [321] et seq.), and must immediately *notify* the seller of any defects in relation to matters covered by representations and warranties. Failing compliance with this examination and notification obligation, the buyer is in principle deemed to have accepted the subject as purchased. Since this statutory regime is often inappropriate for M&A transactions, the parties will typically agree to replace such provisions by giving the right to the buyer to notify any defect during a certain period of time.

[68] Swiss law applicable to sale contracts provides that the seller is not liable for defects about which the buyer had (or should have had) *knowledge* at the time of purchase (*see* paragraphs [329] et seq. and [374]). Thus, if the buyer is aware of a defect when buying a business (e.g., because they discovered a defect when carrying out the due diligence) and the parties do not adopt a different disclosure regime in the share purchase agreement, the buyer should request a purchase price reduction or ask the seller for a specific indemnification covering the matter as they otherwise would be unable to recover damages as a result of a breach of a representation or warranty provided by the seller (*see* paragraph [376]).

[69] Under Swiss property law, the *transfer of legal title* to bearer shares requires the conclusion of a (written or oral) purchase agreement and the transfer of possession of the share certificates (if share certificates have been issued). For title to the shares to validly pass to the buyer, it is also required that the seller be the owner of the shares, or at least that the buyer buys the shares in good faith, i.e., in the belief that the seller owns the shares. It should be noted that recent legislation has effectively abolished bearer shares for private companies as they are only permitted if the company has listed equity securities on a stock exchange or if the bearer shares are structured as intermediated securities and deposited with or entered in the main register of a custodian in Switzerland designated by the company.

[70] The same requirement also applies to the *transfer of registered shares* represented by a certificate, with the additional requirement that the share certificates must be *endorsed* by the seller. If the registered shares are not incorporated in a share certificate, the transfer has to be made in accordance with the rules governing the assignment of claims. This means, among other things, that their assignment must be made in writing and that, if the seller does not have the legitimate right to sell the shares, the buyer will not acquire title to them, even if they are buying them in good faith. *Restricted registered shares* are registered shares that can only be transferred with the approval of the board of directors of the company. With respect to registered shares that are not listed on a stock exchange, the articles of association of the company may provide that the board of directors has the right to refuse to approve the transfer of the shares, either for one of the 'valid causes' set forth in the articles of association, or without cause, provided that the company offers to acquire the shares from the transfer for its own account or for the account of other shareholders or third parties. In each case, the shares must be acquired at their real value at the time of the request for approval. As long as the board directors has not granted its consent, the buyer does not acquire title to the shar and the related rights. Therefore, in the share purchase agreement, the buy should always require as a pre-condition to closing that the board of directo approves the transfer of the purchased restricted registered shares. In the case restricted registered shares listed on a stock exchange, Swiss law provides that th company may refuse to approve a transfer only if the articles of association limit th percentage up to which a shareholder may acquire shares of the company, and suc limit would be exceeded if the contemplated transfer were approved.

[71] Closing a share deal is relatively simple. The shares have to be *surrender* against *payment* of the purchase price. The purchase price is usually paid by wi transfer.

[71a] The parties may now also transfer register value rights. The acts of transf of register value rights are governed by a registration agreement. However, a tran fer must be entered in the register of uncertificated securities, since a register valu right can only be transferred via the register of uncertificated securities. On th execution date, the seller rewrites the register value rights in the register of unce tificated securities to the buyer and submits the extract of the amended register uncertificated securities to the buyer.

Merger

[72] The Merger Act, which provides for two forms of statutory mergers, gover statutory mergers: merger by absorption (*'Absorptionsfusion'*) and merger by comb nation (*'Kombinationsfusion'*). In a *merger by absorption*, one or more companies a dissolved and their business operations are transferred to an already existing com pany. In a *merger by combination*, all companies participating in the merger are di solved and their business operations are transferred to a new company.

[73] In a statutory merger, the assets and liabilities of the transferring compa (i.e., the company that is taken over) will automatically pass to the surviving com pany without any need to comply with the specific requirements for transfer of eac asset or liability (i.e., *principle of universal succession*). However, it is not possible agree on the exclusion of certain assets or liabilities from the merger. The conse of the creditors or debtors is not required and the company which will be disconti ued does not have to be formally liquidated.

[74] As a rule, the shareholders of the transferring company become shareholde of the surviving company *(principle of continuity of membership)*. However, the Merg Act provides that, subject to certain conditions, consideration other than shares i the surviving company can be given to the shareholders of the transferring com pany. The parties to the merger may agree in the merger agreement that th minority shareholders have to accept a cash consideration (or consideration kind) if at least 90% of the votes of the transferring company vote in favour of th merger (squeeze-out merger).

[75] The Merger Act in great detail regulates the *procedure* to be followed for th implementation. The merger agreement must be in writing and must be conclude between the participating companies. It must mainly contain, *inter alia*, the undertaking to merge, a description of the kind of merger (absorption or combination) and of the surviving company, the details of the *exchange ratio for participation* rights and the settlement amount, if any. The supervisory boards of the merging companies must provide for a *merger report* addressed to the shareholders in which they explain and justify the merger. The merger agreement as well as the merger report and merger balance sheet must be audited by a *qualified auditor*, who has to confirm, among other things, that the exchange ratio for the participation rights is fair. The shareholders of the participating companies have the right to review the merger agreement, merger report and audit report as well as the relevant financial statements. The merger must then be *approved by the shareholders' meetings* of all participating companies. In case of an Ltd, such resolution is, in general, passed with at least two-thirds of the votes represented at the shareholders' meeting and the absolute majority of the par value of the shares represented. In case of an LLC, the resolution must, in general, be passed with the consent of at least three-quarters of all partners who must, furthermore, represent at least three-quarters of the company capital. The merger resolution requires the form of a public deed. *Procedural simplifications* are available to parent-subsidiary mergers, mergers between sister companies, and mergers between SMEs. The merger becomes effective when it is entered into the Commercial Register (which is public).

[76] The Merger Act contains provisions for the *protection of creditors*. The respective measures take place after the merger has become effective. In general, the creditors may ask for security of their claims for a period of three months after the effective date of the merger. The merging companies must inform their creditors of this right by way of publication in the Swiss Gazette of Commerce. A number of provisions of the Merger Act are designed to *protect the employees*. The surviving company automatically and as a matter of law becomes the new employer, unless the employee objects. The companies involved in the merger will have to consult the employees prior to the merger becoming effective. If the duty to consult is not complied with, the employees can object to the entry of the merger in the Commercial Register, thus blocking the effective completion of the merger (*see* paragraphs [527] et seq.).

Quasi-Merger (Share for Share Transaction)

[77] In a *quasi-merger*, the acquiring company acquires the shares of the target company from the shareholders in exchange for its own shares, either in full or in part. The quasi-merger is not specifically regulated under Swiss law. If the target company is a privately held company, the general principles of the CO apply. If the target company is a listed Swiss company, the transaction will be subject to the takeover provisions of SESTA. A quasi-merger has a number of advantages, in particular the fact that two companies can be combined under common control without dissolving one of them (as would be the case in a statutory merger). This means that after a quasi-merger all of the companies concerned will continue to hold their rights and liabilities. Goodwill, concessions or other assets are preserved because the target company continues to exist as a legal entity. In contrast to a statutory merger, the acquiring company will not become liable directly for liabilities of t target company. The detailed provisions of the Merger Act that govern statutc mergers do not apply here.

Demergers

[78] The Merger Act provides for two forms of demerger. In the case of a *spin-* (*'Abspaltung'*) two or more companies are formed out of an existing company, pr vided that the existing company continues to exist. In the case of a *split-off* (*'Aufsp tung'*), however, the existing company will be dissolved and its business will transferred to other companies. All shareholders of the transferring company w continue to be shareholders, the allocation being dependent on the form demerger (spin-off or split-off, symmetric or asymmetric demerger). Contrary statutory mergers, the shareholders may not be squeezed-out by way of a cash or kind payment. Once a demerger has been entered in the Commercial Register, t assets and liabilities set forth in the *inventory* are transferred automatically and law. Hence, the demerger is comparable to universal succession characteristics statutory mergers. Contrary to statutory mergers, however, the demerger does n apply to all business assets and liabilities, but only to those listed in the invento (partial universal succession).

[79] The Merger Act in great detail regulates the *procedure* to be followed for t implementation of the demerger. If assets and liabilities are to be transferred existing companies, the supervisory bodies of the companies have to conclude *demerger agreement*. If a company intends to transfer parts of its assets and liabiliti to companies that will be newly established, its supervisory body has to prepare *demerger plan*. Both the demerger agreement and the demerger plan must be writing and have to contain, *inter alia*, an *inventory of the assets and liabilities*, a list the employees to be transferred and details on the exchange ratio for participati rights. The supervisory bodies of the companies involved must provide for demerger report addressed to the shareholders of the companies, providing explanation and the reasons for the demerger. The demerger agreement or, as t case may be, the demerger plan as well as the demerger report and demerger b ance sheet must be *audited* by a particularly qualified auditor, who has to, amo other things, confirm that the exchange ratio for participation rights is fair. Ther after, the shareholders of the companies involved must be granted the opportun to review the demerger agreement or, as the case may be, the demerger pla demerger report and audit report as well as the relevant financial statements. T *demerger resolution* by the shareholders has to be recorded in the form of a pub deed. Procedural simplifications are available for demergers of SMEs.

[80] The Merger Act contains provisions for the *protection of creditors*. The comp nies involved in the demerger must publish the intended demerger in the Sw Gazette of Commerce at least two months prior to the *shareholders'* resolutions a inform the creditors of their right to ask for security of their claims. All compani participating in the demerger are jointly and severally liable for the claims th have been transferred to other companies.

[81] The Merger Act also contains a number of provisions designed to *protect the employees*. These are similar to the provisions governing statutory mergers.

Alternative Demerger Structures

[82] It is worth noting that demergers may not only be accomplished by applying the specifically designed structure and procedures set forth in the Merger Act but also by way of a transfer of the business which is to be *spun-off to a newly created, wholly owned subsidiary* of the demerging company, followed by a distribution in kind (by dividend or capital reduction) of the shares of the new subsidiary to the shareholders of the demerging company. This structure was the usual way of effecting a demerger prior to the entry into force of the Merger Act. The alternative demerger has the advantage that it provides for *less publicity* and, at least in theory, for less creditor protection. It is, however, controversial under Swiss law whether the joint and several liability of the companies participating in the demerger can effectively be avoided by structuring a demerger in the old way.

Transfer of Assets (Asset Deal)

[83] The Merger Act provides that sales of assets and liabilities (asset deals) by entities registered in the Commercial Register can be carried out through a *transfer of assets and liabilities* requiring, essentially, an asset transfer agreement and the filing of the transaction with the Commercial Register (asset transfer). It is resolved by the competent supervisory or management bodies of the companies involved in the transaction and the shareholders in principle have no say in it. Only if all or substantially all assets of the company are sold it would be considered a (factual) liquidation of the company, which will require the shareholders' approval and an amendment of the purpose clause of the articles of association.

[84] The asset transfer agreement requires a written form. A written *inventory* of all assets and liabilities to be transferred has to be drawn up. If real estate is part of the transaction, the parts of the asset transfer agreement referring to the transfer of real estate require a public deed. The minimum requirements of the asset transfer agreement include, *inter alia*, provisions regarding the inventory of assets and liabilities to be transferred, the valuation of the assets and liabilities to be transferred, the consideration and a list of the employment agreements to be transferred. The assets and liabilities specified in the asset transfer agreement will transfer to the buyer as a matter of law. Therefore, the rules that usually govern the transfer of individual assets do not apply. The inventory of assets and liabilities must show a positive balance. It has to be filed with the Commercial Register together with the asset transfer agreement in order for the transfer to be effective. Assets and liabilities not listed in the inventory, including forgotten assets and liabilities, remain with the seller.

Transfer of Contracts

[85] It is still an open question under Swiss law whether contracts listed in the inventory will *transfer automatically* during an asset transfer or whether the *consent* of the counterparties to the contracts is required for the transfer to become effectiv Most practitioners support the concept of an automatic transfer of contract admitting at the very most a right of opposition of the contractual party who doe not agree with the transfer, e.g., in case of a highly personal contract or an abusiv transfer of a contract totally unrelated to the business to be transferred. Non assignment or change of control provisions in a contract could prevent the transfe of such agreements to the buyer and need to be assessed individually in each cas

[86] The common rule applicable to employment agreements applies to the tran fer of employees, i.e., each *employee automatically transfers with the business* to whic they belong. Employees have a right to oppose their transfer to the buyer. Th employees must be *informed* about the planned transaction and have *consultatio rights* if the proposed transfer materially affects their employment rights an duties. The employees may proceed to an injunction against the transferring part and temporarily block the filing process if the information and consultation dutie are not duly complied with. (*See* paragraphs [527] et seq. for more details).

[87] The asset transfer becomes effective upon *filing* of the asset transfer agree ment including the inventory of assets and liabilities with the Commercial Registe Once registered, all documents filed with the Commercial Register can be con sulted by third persons at the Commercial Register, including information abou the valuation of the assets and liabilities and the consideration agreed by the par ties.

Asset Purchase Based on the CO

[88] Prior to the enactment of the Merger Act, asset deals were structured based o the CO as simple sales, whereby assets had to be conveyed and liabilities had to b assumed one by one. This regime of asset deals still exists and is applied quit often, in particular, if the parties wish to *avoid publicity* of the transaction followin the application of the Merger Act. Asset deals are usually agreed in writing. Th parties will have to specify and agree which assets and liabilities are to be tran ferred to the buyer. The formalities have to be observed in respect of each asset an liability to be transferred (principle of '*Singularsukzession*').

2.2.3 Voluntary Codes, Guidelines or Self-Regulation Mechanisms

[89] There are no voluntary codes, guidelines or self-regulation mechanisms tha specifically deal with M&A transactions. It should be noted, however, that there ar regulations which may have an influence on M&A transactions, such as the Swis Code *of Best Practice for Corporate Governance* published by Economiesuisse. I should also be noted that Swiss Private Equity & Corporate Finance Associatio (SECA), for example, publishes *model documentation on transactions in the priva equity sector* that influences practice.

2.3 Relevant Regulatory Authorities

2.3.1 Main Governmental and Regulatory Authorities and Their Responsibility

[90] There are various regulatory authorities that might become involved in M&A deals, depending on the size of the merging companies, their listing on a stock exchange, the business area in which they are active, their holdings of real estate, etc.

[91] In general, *Swiss State Secretariat for Economic Affairs (SECO)* is responsible for negotiating international law disciplines on investment, particularly bilateral investment protection agreements. SECO represents Switzerland in the bodies of international institutions dealing with investment policy and investment law (e.g., WTO, OECD, United Nations Conference on Trade and Development (UNCTAD), etc.). It is also actively involved in the formulation of Swiss investment policy. So far, there are no general restrictions on foreign investments. This has been confirmed recently by the Swiss Government.

[92] SECO is also competent to rule on issues of existing *embargos*. Specific investment restrictions might apply if the government has called for an embargo regarding certain foreign states or individuals.

[93] Compliance with competition law is ensured by the *Swiss Competition Commission (SCC)*. It is an independent federal authority, and its Secretariat is responsible for applying the Anti-Cartel Act. The Commission's tasks include combating harmful cartels, monitoring dominant companies for signs of anticompetitive conduct, enforcing merger control legislation and preventing the imposition of restraints of competition by the state (*see* paragraphs [390] et seq.).

[94] In the case of listed companies, the *Swiss Takeover Board (TOB)* becomes active. It is a Federal Commission established under SESTA which ensures compliance with the rules applicable to public offers (*see* paragraphs [195] et seq.).

[95] Regarding the business areas, there are several authorities that may assume controlling functions. In the financial industry, for example, *FINMA* should be consulted in advance to ensure it does not raise objections to any transaction (*see*, e.g., paragraph [104] or [107]) and revoke previously granted licenses. If real estate is involved, foreign investors, including Swiss companies dominated by persons living abroad, the *Lex Koller authorities* – mainly on the cantonal level – are competent to grant or deny approval of the transaction (*see* paragraphs [118] et seq. and the list with all addresses at the end of the Federal Authority's information leaflet: https://www.bj.admin.ch/dam/data/bj/wirtschaft/grundstueckerwerb/lex-e.pdf).

[96] Under the FMIA, FINMA is also competent to investigate and sanction insider trading and market manipulation by all market participants. It looks into reports from exchanges and foreign supervisory authorities, information obtained in the course of its normal supervision activities and from its own market monitoring. FINMA's efforts are coordinated with the Office of the Attorney General, which is responsible for prosecuting criminal offences involving market abuse.

[97] The respective *cantonal and federal Commercial Registers* are competent to che whether a transaction meets all corporate requirements.

2.3.2 Timing Implications of the Various Governmental Approvals

[98] In most cases, the SCC and/or FINMA require the longest decision periods. I the case of the SCC, decisions are usually rendered between two and ten week while FINMA has various response times, be it as the authority to grant or mainta licenses or as the appellate body for decisions issued by the TOB. The Lex Koll authorities usually take a decision within four weeks after the request was filed.

[99] As in tax matters, it is highly advisable to contact the authorities well i advance and to initiate preliminary talks on the respective subject. This may hel enormously to speed up matters and shorten the authority's response time. Th process is not overly bureaucratic and it is possible to contact the agencies directl However, due to the complexity of these matters, it is advisable to seek legal assi tance when negotiating with the respective government office.

[100] Of course, informal contacts are not appropriate, for example in appella proceedings before FINMA in order to challenge a decision by the TOB or in oth judicial proceedings.

2.4 Controls and Restrictions on Foreign Investment

2.4.1 No Restrictions on Foreign Investment

[101] There are *no general restrictions on foreign investment*. In view of increasir acquisitions especially by Chinese state-owned companies, the government revi ited the question in early 2019 but declined any need for more stringent regul tions for the time being (*see* paragraph [636]). It issued its opinion on 13 Februa 2019 in a 'Report on cross-border investments and investment control'. However, is worth noting that in Switzerland, in contrast to some of its neighbours, mo infrastructure companies such as the mail service, railways, energy producers, gri providers, hospitals and airports are owned by the Confederation, the cantons c the municipalities and are not up for sale, regardless how much money is offere Consequently, in general, it does not make a difference whether a foreign buy intends to acquire a 100% interest or only a partial interest.

[101a] While the Federal Council denied any need to implement an investme control regime on its own, on 3 March 2020, the two chambers of the parliame adopted a contrary motion by a few members. The parliament so commissione the government to prepare a draft act in order to establish a control regime for fo eign investments. So far, since March 2020, the government has not yet presente such draft. Nevertheless, since such adopted motions are binding on the gover ment, Switzerland will receive an investment control regime in the next few year

Defence

[102] There is no specific restriction for foreigners to acquire companies in the *defence sector*. However, if they are deemed to be important such as RUAG Holding AG, the Confederation is the sole shareholder.

Banking

[103] The *Banking Act restricts the acquisition of banks holding a banking license in Switzerland by foreigners*. When a controlling stake in an initially Swiss-controlled bank is transferred to foreign ownership, an additional banking license is required. An *additional license* is also required in the case of changes of foreign shareholders with a qualified participation in a foreign-controlled bank. This latter legal requirement applies to Swiss banks and securities firms as well as to branches of foreign banks and securities firms.

[104] The members of the board and management of a bank in Switzerland must report to FINMA all facts that indicate *foreign control* of the bank or a change of foreign shareholder with a qualified participation. A foreign investor must notify FINMA before directly or indirectly acquiring or selling a qualified participation in a bank organised under Swiss law. In accordance with the principle that shareholders with a qualified participation in a Swiss financial institution or Swiss financial market infrastructure must enjoy a good reputation and their influence must not be detrimental to prudent and sound business operations, natural persons or legal entities who directly or indirectly hold equity interests in the bank of at least 10% of the capital or voting rights or whose business activities can otherwise influence the bank in a significant manner (qualified participation) must guarantee that their influence will not have a negative impact on the bank's prudent and sound business operations.

[105] Swiss banks qualify as *foreign controlled* if foreign shareholders holding qualified participations directly or indirectly hold more than half of the voting rights or exert a controlling influence in any other way. The term 'foreigners' refers to individuals who have neither Swiss citizenship nor hold a Swiss residence permit C. Legal entities are regarded as foreign if their registered office is outside Switzerland or if they are directly or indirectly controlled by foreigners.

[106] FINMA grants an additional banking license subject to the condition that the countries in which the shareholders holding a qualified participation are resident or domiciled guarantee *reciprocal rights*. Reciprocal rights do not have to be verified if international agreements to this effect exist, e.g., with Member States of the WTO. If the transfer to foreign control causes the bank to become part of a financial group or a financial conglomerate, the foreign supervisory authority may need to give its consent and be in a position to ensure consolidated supervision of the group as a whole.

Insurance

[107] Investment by foreigners in insurance companies domiciled in Switzerla is restricted. Any investor who intends to directly or indirectly invest in an insu ance company domiciled in Switzerland must *notify FINMA* if the participati reaches or exceeds 10%, 20%, 33% or 50% of the capital or voting rights of t insurance company. FINMA must be notified each time one of the thresholds reached or exceeded and also in the event of falling below such thresholds. Wh calculating the relevant values, all equity securities that are owned by the benefic owner or confer voting rights on them must be included. In addition to the exe cisable voting rights, all non-exercisable voting rights must be included as well.

[108] *FINMA* may prohibit a participation or subject it to conditions if the natu or scope of the participation could endanger the insurance company or the inte ests of the insured persons. In addition, FINMA also assesses whether the shar holder meets the standards of prudent and sound business operations.

Financial Services

[109] Investment by foreigners in Swiss-domiciled *securities firms* is restricted a the same principles apply as for investments in banks domiciled in Switzerland (above paragraphs [103] et seq.).

[110] In addition, the principle that shareholders with a *qualified participation* in Swiss financial institution or Swiss financial market infrastructure must enjoy good reputation and their influence must not be detrimental to prudent and sou business operations applies (*see* paragraph [104]). FINMA assesses holdings Swiss financial institutions on a case-by-case basis. If FINMA comes to the concl sion that a qualified participation in a Swiss financial institution jeopardises pr dent and sound business operations, it may apply all supervisory instruments accordance with the Financial Market Supervision Act.

Utilities, Energy Markets and Transportation

[111] There is no formal restriction for foreign investors to acquire holdings infrastructure, energy or transportation companies. However, the government h earmarked the industries or key companies that provide vital services and usua reserves a significant participation for itself. This can be done at the municip cantonal or federal level. For example, energy companies can be organised as public-law entity or a private stock corporation. In the first case, no acquisition possible by foreigners due to the legal structure of the entity. In the latter case, t government is either not interested in keeping it in Swiss hands or reserves a co trolling stake for itself which is not up for sale. All other shares can in principle al be bought by foreign investors.

[112] To provide an example, most of the Swiss railway infrastructure belongs the Federal Railway Company, which is organised as a special stock corporati under the Swiss Federal Railway Act. The Confederation is the shareholder, but it can decide to sell part of the shares. However, the Confederation must at all times remain the majority shareholder in terms of capital and votes. If the Confederation lawfully decides to sell part of the shares, no restriction applies.

2.4.2 Restrictions on Foreign Directors or Managers

Local Representatives

[113] Swiss company law (as part of the CO) requires that the company is represented by and can act through directors or other signatories living in Switzerland. Therefore, at least one person authorised to sign with sole signature or two persons with joint signature rights must have their legal residence in Switzerland (*see* paragraphs [27] and [34]). It is not required that they are appointed as directors in case of an Ltd or as managers if it is an LLC. In addition, there are also no citizenship requirements for the officers of any company form.

Government Officials on a Supervisory Basis as an Exception

[114] Once all permits and licenses are in place, no presence of any government official is required for supervision. In the rare case of supervision, e.g., in the financial sector, companies are only required to file reports and to comply with the relevant ordinances issued by the authority.

[115] The only exceptions where officials are required as representatives include companies that perform services relevant to the public, are owned by communities or have significant public investment.

2.4.3 No Permit to Trade for a Foreign-Owned Company, in General

[116] Generally speaking, foreign-owned companies are not subject to a special trade licence. However, issues arise depending on the industry (e.g., banks structured as a subsidiary of a foreign financial institution are subject to certain regulations, companies in the defence sector must observe other special restrictions, real estate companies may need a permit for each acquisition).

No Minimum Capital Requirements (or Capital Import Requirements) for Foreign-Owned Companies

[117] There are certain minimum capital requirements exceeding the ones set forth generally in company law (e.g., for banks), but none is applicable to a company solely due to its foreign ownership.

Restrictions on Acquisition of Real Estate by Persons Abroad

Principles of the Lex Koller

[118] The Lex Koller restricts foreign investments in Swiss real estate. Accordin to the Lex Koller (and the accompanying federal ordinance in force), the acquis tion of real estate in Switzerland by persons abroad requires *authorisation from th competent authority* of the canton in which the real estate is situated. It is the canton primary responsibility to enforce the Lex Koller, and therefore, up to the authorit granted to them, to decide whether such authorisation may be granted, provide that this is permitted by the Lex Koller and, if applicable, by cantonal law. It i important to know that in principle, in terms of the authorisation requirement an with regard to the granting of such authorisation, it is immaterial whether the re estate has previously been in foreign hands or what the legal basis for the real estat acquisition is.

Conditions for a Transaction Subject to Authorisation Requirement

Overview

[119] A legal transaction requires authorisation under the Lex Koller, if (cumula tively, and always within the special meaning of this law) (i) the subject acquiring i a *person abroad*, (ii) the acquisition object is *real estate*, (iii) the legal right the subjec *acquires* to the object is considered an acquisition, and (iv) *no exemptions* to th authorisation requirements apply.

Person Abroad

[120] 'Persons abroad' as defined by the Lex Koller are on the one hand foreig *natural persons* residing outside of Switzerland, and on the other foreign natura persons domiciled in Switzerland who are citizens of neither an European Commu nity (EC) nor an EFTA country nor the United Kingdom and who do not have valid residence permit (the so-called C permit). Considered to be 'persons abroac are also all *legal entities* that have their registered office abroad, regardless whethe they are Swiss-owned, as well as legal entities domiciled in Switzerland that are con trolled by persons abroad, unless they are listed on the Swiss stock exchange or ar investment funds regularly traded on off-exchange markets. Foreign control i given under the Lex Koller if more than one-third of a company's capital or mor than one-third of the voting rights are controlled by persons abroad or if a perso abroad has granted substantial loans to the company. Last, but not least, *trusts* c *fiduciaries* who acquire real estate on behalf of persons abroad are also considered t be persons abroad.

Real Estate

[121] 'Real estate' in the very broad definition of the Lex Koller entails all kinds of property held directly or indirectly, in sole ownership, joint or co-ownership, condominium ownership, and usufruct, such as single-family dwellings or apartment houses, owner-occupied flats or building land. Even a leasehold or any other right to real estate is considered to be 'real estate' if the entitled person (for instance, the lessee) holds a position similar to that of a property owner. It is highly relevant to know, however, that the acquisition of real estate *does not require authorisations if* it is *used for commercial purposes* ('business property'), i.e., for permanent business establishments such as factories, warehouse facilities, mines, retail premises or shopping malls, offices, hotels, restaurants, workshops, doctor's practices. Such business property can also be purchased solely as an investment, and the investor can also acquire other rights to such property, for instance, building rights, a right of first refusal, a repurchase right, a mortgage note or financing rights. However, the construction, rental or leasing of housing is not recognised as a permanent business activity in the above sense and the acquisition of real estate for such purposes is prohibited as there are no grounds for granting authorisation. Hotel-based accommodation, on the other hand, is considered to be a commercial purpose, so that such property can be acquired or built without approval under the Lex Koller. Under certain exceptional circumstances, living space may be acquired by persons abroad in connection with their permanent business establishment in Switzerland. It must, however, be mentioned that in this context prior authorisation is principally required for the acquisition of undeveloped land in residential, industrial or commercial zones, unless the construction of a building for which no such authorisation is required, for instance, a main residence or permanent business establishment, is commenced within approximately one year, or it is otherwise used as a permanent establishment (PE) property (e.g., storage space, car park, access road), or it can be regarded as a permissible land reserve. Vacant buildings which no longer serve the purpose of exercising any economic activity are regarded as undeveloped land. The hoarding of land, even if it is not located in a residential zone but in an industrial or commercial zone, is also considered an impermissible capital investment.

Acquisition

[122] An 'acquisition' as broadly defined by the Lex Koller entails *any transaction*, regardless of its legal basis, which transfers actual financial control of real estate. This may be through a purchase, a call or put option, a pre-emption right, or a right of repurchase. This does not, however, only comprise Land Register entries, but also includes the *purchase of shares* (even just one share or non-voting shares) in a non-listed legal entity or participation in a company without legal personality whose purpose is to acquire and/or own real estate. Even the *financing* of a purchase or construction of real estate where the agreements, the size of the loans or the financial circumstances of the debtor put the buyer or the contractor into a special dependency on the creditor, is considered an acquisition.

No Further Exemptions Apply

[123] Regardless of the aforementioned, certain persons are exempt from th requirements to obtain authorisation mentioned under paragraphs [120]–[122 This includes legal heirs under Swiss law (by legal succession or by will), perso acquiring real estate as part of an estate, relatives in line of ascent or descent fro the person disposing of the property, and their spouse or registered partner, buye who already hold an interest in the property (by joint ownership, co-ownership, o other condominium owners), in certain particular cases, real estate owners fro abroad for smaller units, and cross-border EC and EFTA commuters for a second ary residence in the area of their workplace.

Procedures

Procedure for Establishing Authorisation

[124] If the authority involved in the transaction, e.g., the Land Registry (in th case of direct land transactions), the Commercial Registry (for the acquisition o company shares) or the Auctioneers' Office (for debt collection and bankrupt auctions of land or shares) cannot immediately rule out the possibility of a transa tion requiring prior authorisation, they will refer the buyer to another authori where they must apply for authorisation or a declaration that no authorisation required. The authorisation body will then take a decision which can be appeale before a cantonal appeals body, whose ruling thereon can be appealed before th Swiss Federal Supreme Court (SFSC).

Grounds for Authorisation

[125] The grounds for authorisation provided in the Lex Koller and, as appropr ate, in cantonal legislation, are very limited. For example, banks and insuran companies with a permit to operate in Switzerland may, under certain circum stances, acquire real estate as a result of foreclosing a mortgage. Furthermor authorisation may also be granted if the acquisition of real estate is used by a Swi business for pension scheme operations benefiting personnel employed in Switze land. Last but not least, authorisation for the acquisition of apartments in holid resorts may be granted under cantonal provisions permitting an annual quota.

Legal Consequences of Violating the Lex Koller

[126] In terms of civil law, transactions requiring authorisation are invalid un authorisation is obtained. The violation of the Lex Koller may also have crimin consequences, which are punishable with a prison sentence or fine.

Conclusions for the M&A Practice

[127] In cases where the authorisation requirement cannot be ruled out immed ately, the acquisition agreement usually makes confirmation by the canton authority that the acquisition is not subject to authorisation or, in cases where th authorisation is necessary, the granting of the authorisation to acquire a condition precedent to closing. With regard to the timeline of the closing process, it must be emphasised that it takes a considerable amount of time (usually more than two months) to obtain the final confirmation that no authorisation is required or the authorisation itself.

2.5 Incentives for Foreign Investment

2.5.1 No General Restrictions on Foreign Investors

[128] The payment of dividends abroad and the repatriation of profits and/or the proceeds of liquidation and sale are permitted, but are subject to *tax* (*see* paragraphs [449] et seq.), in particular withholding tax (WHT) (*see* paragraphs [499] et seq.)

[129] The *collateralisation of debt financing* of an M&A deal is explained under paragraphs [173] et seq. There are no restrictions on the payment of interest on foreign loans or fees and charges for IP or technology transfer to foreign companies. Needless to say, taxes imposed have to be observed (*see* paragraphs [486] et seq. and [511] et seq., [515] et seq. and [519] et seq.).

[130] There are *no relevant exchange control* or currency regulations affecting foreign investors. Transfers of funds to foreign lenders for payment of interest or repayment of capital are not controlled. Domestic companies can hold off-shore bank accounts.

[131] One restriction has to be mentioned, which, however, similarly applies to Swiss and foreign investors: *radio and television* enterprises require a *concession* issued by Swiss Federal Department of Environment, Transport, Energy and Communications (DETEC). The transfer of a concession requires the prior written approval of DETEC because transfer of a concession includes a change of ownership with respect to more than 20% of the capital, the shares or the voting rights of the concession holder.

2.5.2 Government Guarantees Against Expropriation or Nationalisation

Guarantees Against Expropriation or Nationalisation

Constitutional Guarantee of Ownership and Its Restrictions

[132] The Swiss constitution guarantees the right to own property as a fundamental right (guarantee of ownership). Nevertheless, there are certain restrictions of this fundamental right, with expropriation being the most severe restriction of the individual property rights permitted under Swiss law. Nationalisation, i.e., the transformation of a private company into a state-owned enterprise, is unknown to the Swiss legal system. However, in recent times, certain representatives of left-wing political parties have occasionally demanded the nationalisation of major Sw banks.

[133] Like any restriction of a fundamental right guaranteed by the constitutio an *expropriation* always needs to meet the following requirements: it (i) must have legal basis permitting the restriction, (ii) must be justified in the public interest for the protection of the fundamental rights of others, (iii) must be proportiona and (iv) may not undermine the essence of the fundamental right. Additionally, t constitutional provision demands full compensation for compulsory purchases property and any restriction on ownership equivalent to compulsory purchase.

Expropriation Procedures

[134] As a federal state, Switzerland has expropriation laws on the federal as w as the underlying cantonal level. These expropriation laws in combination with t respective regulations requiring the expropriation (e.g., railway or nature prote tion laws) serve as the legal basis for expropriations. Expropriation under Swiss la is mainly an instrument for procuring land *for public purposes*, thus it mostly targe real estate. The Federal Expropriation Act does not provide a legal basis for t expropriation of movable goods, while some cantonal expropriation laws do so.

[135] The expropriation procedure is divided into an administrative and a judic procedure. The *administrative procedure* deals with questions of the validity, subje and extent of the expropriation whereas the *judicial procedure* follows the decision the administrative procedure and deals with the appropriate compensation for t loss of property. Generally, the expropriation procedure is highly complex a requires substantial financial effort by the government body planning to underta the expropriation, thus making expropriations rather uncommon.

Taking Security over Immovable Property by Foreign Lenders

[136] The *Lex Koller restricts* foreign investments in Swiss real estate by stating th acquisition of real estate in Switzerland by persons abroad requires, under certa conditions, authorisation from the appropriate authority of the canton in which t real estate is situated. Where the agreements, the size of the loans or the financ circumstances of the debtor put the buyer or the contractor in a special depe dency relationship to the (foreign) creditor, even the financing of purchase or co struction of real estate is considered an acquisition as defined by the Lex Koller a may therefore require an authorisation.

[137] Since, however, the agreement according to which the security right over re property is to accrue to the creditor as property is invalid by law in Switzerland, t foreign creditor does not acquire an ownership-like position in the security rig over real property, nor is there any particular relationship of dependency betwe the buyer of the financed property/debtor on the one hand and the (foreign) cre tor on the other. For this reason, it is generally permissible in Switzerland finance the acquisition of real estate through foreign loans secured by mortgag on immovable property, and foreign creditors may secure their loans with a mo gage on a Swiss immovable property.

2.5.3 No Investment Incentives Available to Foreign Investors

[138] Switzerland does not have special economic zones or a free zone, neither for domestic businesses nor for foreign investors. However, *duty-free warehouses* exist and are used to temporarily store goods on which no tax or duty has been paid. Import duties only need to be paid on goods destined for sale after the end of stockpiling in a duty-free warehouse. Such warehousing, consequently, is used for highly taxed goods, goods subject to a quota and/or goods whose end-use is not yet certain. The duty-free warehouses are operated by private warehousing companies but have a public character and are open to all interested parties.

[139] A Swiss tax reform to enter into force on 1 January 2020 has abolished the tax privileges in relation to the *holding company* regime and the *domicile* (administration, mixed or auxiliary) *company* regime. Such regimes will be replaced by new internationally accepted tax measures. A so-called patent box at cantonal level will provide tax relief for income from IP resulting from research and development, and the cantons may introduce additional tax relief for R&D expenditures by introducing a higher tax deduction for research and development costs at the cantonal level. Furthermore, under certain conditions the cantons may introduce a notional interest deduction on equity capital and a reduction of cantonal capital tax on qualifying participations, patents and comparable rights. Companies that were previously taxed under a privileged holding or domicile regime will maintain their existing level of taxation for a transitional period of five years, i.e., until the end of 2024. For further tax incentives, *see* paragraphs [442] et seq.

2.6 Specific Issues of Company and Security Law

(by Reto Arpagaus, Barbara Jecklin)

[140] In the following, no differentiations are made between the various company forms, unless it is explicitly mentioned. Therefore, when explanations for the Ltd are given, they also apply for the LLC, when the terms 'shareholders' or 'board of directors' are used, they also stand for partners or general managers (*see* paragraphs [24] et seq. and [32] et seq.).

2.6.1 Shareholder Approval Rights

[141] Shareholder approval rights vary, contingent upon the structure of the planned transaction.

[142] In the event of a *merger*, the board of directors, *as a rule*, must submit the merger agreement to the shareholders of both the acquiring and the transferring company for approval. Such shareholders' resolution requires, as a rule, the consent of at least (i) two-thirds of the nominal value represented at the shareholders' meeting and (ii) the absolute majority of the nominal value of the shares represented by them, if such shares are entitled to vote. If the takeover of an Ltd by an LLC results in an obligation to make a supplementary capital contribution or another personal obligation, as is standard for an LLC, but not for an Ltd, a affected new shareholders must approve the merger. Other quorum requiremen may apply, depending on the specific form of the legal entities involved.

[143] An exception to the approval requirement exists for so-called simplifie mergers. If the acquiring company owns all the shares with voting rights of th transferring company, or if a legal entity, an individual or a legally or contractuall connected group of persons owns all the shares with voting rights of both mergin companies, neither the shareholders of the transferring nor those of the acquirin company need to pass a merger resolution. Similar alleviations apply if the acqui ing company owns at least 90% of the shares with voting rights of the transferrin company.

[144] On the other hand, the merger requires the approval of at least 90% c shareholders with voting rights if the merger agreement provides only for cash o other compensation for the shareholders without any choice to opt for continue membership rights.

[145] By contrast, as a rule, neither the *purchase* or *sale of shares* (*see* paragraphs [66 et seq.) nor the *transfer of assets and liabilities* of a company (*see* paragraphs [83] e seq.) requires a shareholders' resolution as a condition precedent to closing. Suc restriction, however, may indirectly result from a limitation of the directors' repre sentation power: a transfer agreement must not qualify as the return of a capit contribution to a shareholder and has to, if the transaction results de facto in liqu dation or change of purpose, satisfy the respective majorities for such resolution.

2.6.2 Directors' Duties

[146] The directors of a company engaged in a *merger* transaction (*see* paragraph [72] et seq.) are required to prepare a written merger agreement and a merge report and hold those documents available for inspection by interested sharehold ers of all involved companies. Between the conclusion of the merger agreemen and the shareholders' resolution (if any), the directors of each company bear a information duty vis-à-vis the directors of the other companies involved about sig nificant changes in the assets or liabilities of a company.

[147] If the merger results in a transfer of employment agreements, the directo must inform the respective employees' representation body or the employee about the purpose and consequences of such transfer for the employees, prior t the shareholders' resolution (*see* paragraph [531]). Further, the articles of associ tion may require the directors' approval as a condition precedent to the transfer shares that may only be refused in certain limited circumstances (*see* paragrap [25]).

[148] After the merger agreement has been signed, or after the shareholders hav passed the merger resolution (if any), the directors must apply for the registratio of the merger with the Commercial Register, upon which the merger becom legally effective. Subsequently, the directors have to notify potential creditors of th merger by three publications in the Swiss Gazette of Commerce, unless an audito confirms the non-existence of claims. Any claims of creditors of the merging companies must be secured or satisfied within three months after the effective date of the transaction if the creditors so request, unless the directors can demonstrate that the fulfilment of such claims is not jeopardised by the merger.

[149] *Specific duties* in case of hostile transactions exist for public takeovers (*see* paragraphs [192] et seq.), but general obligations of the directors may result from their duties to due diligence, to equal treatment of all shareholders, and to safeguard the interests of the company in good faith.

2.6.3 Form of Consideration

[150] In a *merger* transaction, the acquiring company has to provide consideration to the shareholders of the transferring company. For that purpose, the acquiring company may increase its share capital by way of an ordinary or authorised capital increase (absorption merger) or by incorporation of a new company (combination merger), pursuant to the legal requirements thereto. Besides the most common possibility of a share capital increase by contribution of cash, an acquiring company may also issue new shares for a non-cash consideration, such as assets or services, or convert freely disposable equity.

[151] A *contribution in kind* within a merger transaction is, at least insofar as a merger resolution was executed, exempt from certain requirements, i.e., it does not need (i) an agreement concerning the contribution in kind, (ii) a capital increase report, (iii) an audit thereof, (iv) a confirmation of free disposability of such assets, and (v) a publication of the contribution in kind in the articles of association. Further, the required merger resolution does not have to include any statements regarding the subscription of the shares. However, identical to other capital increases, the directors must execute a declaratory resolution on the merger-related capital increase and the amendment of the articles of association in the form of a notarial deed. The shares issued for a non-cash contribution in kind are not restricted subsequently.

2.6.4 Completion Formalities

[152] In addition to a written *merger agreement* and a *merger report*, Swiss law requires the preparation of an *interim balance sheet*, if on the date the merger agreement is concluded, the relevant balance sheet dates back more than six months, or if since the date of the last balance sheet, important changes have occurred in the assets and liabilities of the involved companies. An approved auditor must *audit* the agreement, the report as well as the interim balance sheet.

[153] The shareholders' resolution approving the merger (if any) requires a *notarial certification* (*'öffentliche Beurkundung'*). The presence of a notary is therefore mandatory during the adoption of the resolution.

[154] A *transfer of assets and liabilities* pursuant to the Merger Act does not require the preparation of a report or an audit. Since it does not require a resolution by the general meeting of shareholders, the *transfer agreement* itself must be *certified* by a notary to the extent it comprises the transfer of real estate. It is sufficient to dra up a single public deed, even if several properties located in different cantons a transferred. With regard to the transfer of assets and liabilities, a *written invento* has to be compiled.

[155] SMEs are exempt from various legal requirements, in particular from th execution of a merger report, the audit thereof as well as the inspection procedur if all shareholders so approve.

[156] In certain instances, e.g., if the M&A transaction involves financial/insuran institutions (*see also* paragraphs [103] et seq.), the new shareholder(s), new boar member(s) and new member(s) of senior management may *need to pass certain te* before being allowed to assume the position (*'Erfordernis der Gewähr einwandfrei Geschäftsführung'*) (*see also* paragraph [110]).

[157] To complete a transaction, the parties may further have to discharge *notific tion obligations*, e.g., in relation to the financial supervision authority (*see* para graphs [103] et seq. and [107] et seq.), or seek *approval or clearance* from regulato bodies, e.g., from the Swiss (and/or a foreign) competition authority (*see* para graphs [392] et seq. and [245] et seq.).

[158] If the transaction includes the transfer of Swiss real estate, the parties ma need approval by the competent cantonal authority due to the Lex Koller (*see* para graphs [118] et seq.).

2.6.5 Costs and Fees

[159] Excluding *professional advisory fees*, costs and fees will arise as a result of th legally required *audit* of the merger agreement, report and interim balance shee the *notarial certification* of the merger resolution (if any) or the transfer agreeme in the sense of Articles 69 et seq. Merger Act as well as the *registration* with the Com mercial Register. Additional costs will arise if the transaction requires approval c clearance from governmental authorities like regulatory bodies, competitic authorities, etc.

[160] If the target is a listed company, *disclosure obligations* of the parties may aris with the acquisition or disposal of the following holdings of shares: a person wh directly, indirectly or jointly together with third parties acquires listed shares in Swiss company and thereby reaches or exceeds the thresholds of 3%, 5%, 10 15%, 20%, 25%, 33 ⅓%, 50% or 66 ⅔% of the voting rights has to notify the com pany and the stock exchange where the shares are listed (*see* paragraphs [193] an [251]). The same applies in the event of the disposal of shares where the particip tion after the sale of shares falls below the respective thresholds. Companies who shares are listed on a stock exchange (e.g., the SIX Swiss Exchange) are obliged disclose sales and purchases of businesses pursuant to the rules on Ad hoc publici if the transaction is of a size which can result in a material change in market price

2.6.6 Dividends

[161] Under Swiss law, dividends may only be paid out of *distributable profits* and *special reserves*, after having made the legally required *allocations to reserves*. Before distributing dividends, 5% of the yearly profits need to be allocated to the legal reserves until the reserves amount to 20% of the company's paid-up share capital ('first allocation'). In addition, unless the company qualifies as a holding company, 10% of the amounts distributed as a dividend need to be budgeted as legal reserves, provided this equals more than 5% of the share capital ('second allocation').

[162] Again with the exception of holding companies, the legal reserves cannot be distributed to shareholders as long as they do not exceed 50% of the share capital of the company. In addition to reserves stipulated by law, the company's articles of association may provide for further-reaching regulations.

[163] There are no specific restrictions on a domestic company's ability to distribute dividends, whether to domestic shareholders or to foreign shareholders, nor are there corporate restrictions to repatriate dividends to a foreign owner.

2.6.7 Acquisition of Own Shares

[164] Under Swiss law, a company may acquire its own shares provided that (i) the funds needed for the purchase of its own shares qualify as freely disposable equity capital and (ii) the combined nominal value of all such shares does not exceed *10%* of the share capital. A transaction may exceed the latter limitation only if the directors could not foresee the merger resolution's non-compliance therewith, but in no case longer than two years.

[165] The *voting rights*, and rights related thereto, of the company's own shares are *suspended*. Besides, the company must set aside an amount equivalent to the cost of acquiring its own shares as a *separate reserve*.

[166] A company cannot circumvent such restrictions through the acquisition of shares by a majority-owned subsidiary that is subject to the same restrictions and consequences. Further restrictions may result from the equal treatment principle: a company must offer identical commercial conditions to all shareholders and must make a restricted purchase offer to only one category or an individual shareholder for objective reasons.

[167] Under Swiss company law (as part of the CO), a company cannot legally commit to redeem shares and to refund the paid capital contribution to the respective shareholder(s). The cancellation of shares is only possible by means of a formal capital decrease.

2.6.8 Corporate Veil and the Piercing Thereof

[168] Swiss law generally recognises *the legal independence* of a controlled subsidiary despite its lack of economic independence. Consequently, a parent company is, as a rule, not liable for debts or other liabilities of their subsidiaries. However, case law provides for the piercing of such corporate veil and liability of a controlling pare company in *exceptional circumstances based on the principle of good faith*, i.e., if respe ing the legal independence will result in an abuse of rights. However, the thresho is high for such liability. For example, case law held a parent company liak because its business conduct led creditors to believe that a certain subsidiary w incorporated into the parent company (which it was not). In addition, a pare company may be liable to the extent that it was actively involved in a transaction a shareholder. However, such liability is limited to damages arising out of t respective transaction by an intentional or negligent breach of duty.

2.6.9 Insolvency

[169] A *company in the status of liquidation* may participate in a merger as a transfe ring company, as long as the company has not yet commenced with the distributi of assets. A company (i) that no longer has assets equal to at least one half of t amount of its paid-in share capital and legal reserves or (ii) whose liabilities exce its assets may only merge with another company if the acquiring company h unrestricted disposable equity to the extent of the underfunding or the surplus the liabilities in excess of the assets. This latter requirement does not apply to t extent the creditors of the merging companies agree that their claims will be su ordinated to any other claims by other creditors.

[170] A transfer of assets and liabilities may be performed if the transferring co pany is in liquidation, suffers from a loss of capital or has more liabilities th assets. The previous debtor (transferring company) remains jointly and severa liable with the new debtor (acquiring company) for three years for debts incurr prior to the transfer of assets and liabilities.

2.6.10 Choice of Law and Jurisdiction or Arbitration

[171] Choice of law, jurisdiction and arbitration clauses are standard and wide used in Swiss M&A transaction practice. Such clauses are recognised and enforc able (*see also* paragraphs [373] et seq.). Except for the requirement that a merg agreement must comply with the mandatory provisions of the Swiss company la applicable to the companies involved, the merger agreement may be governed the law chosen by the parties. The same applies to the agreement for the transfer assets and liabilities. *Typically*, however, these types of agreements are subject *Swiss law if Swiss companies are involved.*

[172] Acquisition agreements usually contain a choice of law provision as well a jurisdiction clause. The parties may also agree to submit their disputes to an ar tral tribunal.

2.6.11 Financial Assistance

[173] The *granting of security* of any type and over any asset by members of the target group securing a loan made to the acquiring company may raise *financial assistance* issues.

[174] Swiss law does not provide for explicit provisions on financial assistance. However, based on general principles of Swiss company law, a company is prevented from making payments to its direct or indirect shareholders, unless such payment is made (i) in the form of a dividend, (ii) at arm's lengths conditions, or (iii) in the course of a formal reduction of its nominal capital. Other acts having a similar effect (such as the provision of security or an indemnity for the benefit of its direct or indirect shareholder) are subject to the same principles as an actual payment. Thus, to the extent the provision of an 'up-stream' security (i.e., security for obligations of a direct or indirect shareholder of the security provider) or 'cross-stream' security (i.e., security for obligations of a sister company of the security provider) cannot be considered to be made at arm's-length terms, such security, in order to be validly established, should be treated like a dividend distribution, which requires compliance with certain formal requirements. Likewise, the related enforcement proceeds which can be used by the secured party to satisfy its claims are to be *limited to the freely disposable equity* of the security provider which could be distributed as dividend to the shareholder (*see* paragraphs [161] et seq.) at the time of the enforcement of the security, which may considerably limit the value of such 'up/cross-stream' security for the secured party. Also, the payment of up-stream guarantees or the use of enforcement proceeds from an up- or cross-stream security, respectively, is subject to tax implications, in particular to Swiss WHT (*see also* paragraphs [511] et seq.).

[175] Swiss law does not provide for any 'whitewash' procedures or similar measures to avoid or mitigate the consequences of an 'up-' or 'cross-stream' security and there are *no safe-haven* or similar rules as to what conditions are to be considered at arm's length for intra-group security. However, while there is little practical guidance by Swiss courts, Swiss practice has developed *certain best practice standards* in order to ensure the validity of an 'up/cross-stream' security, including, among other things, (i) inclusion of explicit financial assistance wording in the purpose clause of the articles of association of the Swiss security provider, (ii) formal approval of the grant of security not only by the board of directors but also by the shareholders of the security provider, and (iii) inclusion of a Swiss limitation clause in the security agreement, limiting the use of the enforcement proceeds for the satisfaction of the secured claim to the freely distributable reserves of the Swiss security provider at the time of enforcement.

2.6.12 Security Interests

Types of Security

[176] The exact scope of the Swiss security package in an acquisition finance tran action is determined on a case-by-case basis, but typically includes guarantees a well security over shares, receivables, real estate, bank accounts, and occasionally I rights of certain group companies. It has to be noted that the taking of securit over Swiss real estate by foreign secured parties may be limited due to the Lex Ko ler (cf. paragraph [136]).

[177] The *type of security* and perfection mechanics depend on the asset involve and the most customary forms of security are pledges (mostly used for shares), security transfer of legal title to certain assets ('*Sicherungsübereignung*') or a securit assignment of claims ('*Sicherungszession*') (which are mostly used for mortgage ce tificates or receivables), or mortgages over real estate, aircraft and ships.

[178] Perfection of security over most tangible movable property requires th transfer of physical possession of the security asset to the secured party. Conse quently, upon perfection of the security, the security provider is not in a positio anymore to dispose of and use, such assets. Thus, for practical purposes, the prc vision of security over operational movable property (such as inventory, machiner etc.) is not very common in Switzerland.

[179] In addition to security over specific assets, Swiss law knows two differer types of instruments for a '*personal guarantee*' by a security provider, the first on being an abstract guarantee undertaking which is independent of the underlyin secured obligation, and the second one being a suretyship which is of ancillar nature and depends on the validity of the underlying obligation, allowing the gua antor to raise all objections and defences that are also available to the creditor c the secured obligation.

[180] The concept of floating charge or similar charge over all assets of the secu rity provider is not known under Swiss law. This is primarily due to the requiremer of Swiss law that assets subject to security must be sufficiently specified or specif able. Also, the perfection requirement for movable goods (*see* above) would rende such floating charge impracticable.

[181] Swiss law does not know a private or public centralised registry for registra tion of security in general. With the exception of security over real property, ai craft, ships or cattle, which must be recorded in the relevant public register, securit interests do not need to be registered in order to be validly perfected. Howeve depending on the involved asset it might be advisable to have certain securit interests registered (if a relevant register is available) or notified for transparency disclosure purposes, e.g., in order for such security to become enforceable towarc good faith third parties.

Enforcement

[182] To enforce a security, the secured claim must be due. The relevant security agreement can set out additional conditions for the enforcement of the security, such as a specified event of default in respect of the secured obligation.

[183] Unless bankruptcy has been declared, a secured party benefitting from a pledge can enforce its security either (i) through *formal proceedings* pursuant to the Swiss Debt Enforcement and Bankruptcy Act (DEBA) (*see also* paragraphs [366] et seq.) or (ii) – provided this has been agreed between the parties – by way of *private enforcement* (*'Privatverwertung'*). However, in a bankruptcy context, pledged assets form part of the bankruptcy estate as a result of which a pledged asset has to be delivered to the bankruptcy administrator (or receiver, to use another term) who will liquidate the security and hand over the realisation proceeds (net of costs for the bankruptcy administrator and up to the secured amount) to the secured party with a priority over the other creditors. As an exception, private enforcement remains permissible even in a bankruptcy scenario for pledges over book-entry / intermediated securities with a value which can be determined objectively.

[184] To the extent the security was provided in a form transferring legal title to the security assets to the secured party (i.e., by way of security assignment or security transfer), enforcement can only be made by way of private enforcement and the opening of bankruptcy proceedings does not impact the secured party's related rights. However, any surplus resulting from the private enforcement must be turned over to the bankruptcy estate.

[185] There is a general preference in the market for private enforcement as the involvement of the authorities in formal enforcement proceedings may result in a significant slowdown of the realisation process and may also lead to a less favourable outcome in respect of the realised enforcement profit.

[186] An enforcement of security outside of formal proceedings, i.e., by *private enforcement* can take place by private sale, public auction or public offering. If there is a market value of the assets (e.g., listed securities), the secured party may privately enforce the security by purchasing the assets subject to security and applying the proceeds to its claim. However, appropriation without proper accounting of the value of the relevant security asset against the secured obligations is prohibited under Swiss law in all forms of private enforcement. In addition, a secured party is liable to the security provider if the security is not being enforced in good faith (e.g., by a sale below fair market value).

[187] The usual form of *realisation by the bankruptcy administrator* pursuant to the DEBA is a sale of the pledged assets in a public auction. Under certain instances, e.g., for assets with a market price or assets traded on an exchange or in respect of perishable goods, a sale without public auction is possible.

Clawback

[188] Based on the DEBA, the following three types of transactions that were carried out prior to the opening of bankruptcy proceedings may be challenged and set aside by the court. The length of the suspect period in relation to such avoidance preferences depends on the nature of the transaction challenged.

[189] *'Avoidance of gratuitous transactions'*; i.e., gifts and other transactions made fre of charge or without adequate consideration, which were entered into by the debto or the security provider, respectively, within one year prior to the opening of bank ruptcy proceedings.

[190] *'Avoidance due to over-indebtedness'*; i.e., certain acts carried out by the debto or security provider, respectively, within one year from the opening of bankrupt proceedings, while it is over-indebted, including (i) the granting of collateral fo previously unsecured debt; (ii) the settlement of debt by unusual means of pa ment, and (iii) the repayment of a claim not yet due. To the extent the beneficia of such payment or collateral, respectively, was unaware and could not have bee aware of the financial situation of the debtor, such transaction cannot be cha lenged.

[191] *'Avoidance for intent'*; i.e., any act carried out by the debtor or security pro vider, respectively, during five years before the opening of bankruptcy proceedin that had the purpose (apparent for the other party) of disadvantaging creditors preferring certain creditors to the detriment of others.

2.7 Specific Rules on Public Takeovers

(by Pascal Rüedi)

2.7.1 Scope of Application of the Swiss Takeover Rules

Principles on Public Takeovers

[192] Swiss legislation on public takeovers aims to have a neutral impact on th market, i.e., public takeover offers are neither promoted nor prevented by the Swi takeover rules. The objective of the rules on public takeover offers is to ensure th a shareholder of a target company is able to make an *undistorted decision* as whether to accept a public takeover offer and to ensure the functioning of the ma ket. The objectives are based on the fundamental principles of transparency, fai ness, equal treatment of shareholders and protection of minorities.

Scope of Application

Public Tender Offers for Equity Securities of Listed Companies

[193] The Swiss rules on public takeovers apply to public takeover offers relating equity securities of companies (target companies) (i) with their *registered office Switzerland* and whose securities are *at least partly listed* on a stock exchange in Swi zerland (i.e., SIX Swiss Exchange or BX Swiss) or (ii) with their registered offi abroad whose equity securities are in part mainly listed in Switzerland. The ter

'listed shares' refers to shares which are admitted to trading with the consent of the target company.

[194] Contrary to the unambiguous wording of the law, the TOB is of the opinion that – under certain circumstances – the rules may also apply to public offers to buy equity securities of issues with *no listed securities*. This is the case, for example, if the securities were delisted for the purpose of circumventing the Swiss takeover rules.

Public Offer

[195] *Offers publicly made* to purchase or exchange equity securities trigger the application of the Swiss rules on takeovers. A publicly made announcement or press release on the intent to acquire or exchange equity securities qualifies as a public offer as defined by the Swiss rules on public takeovers only if it includes a sufficiently specific invitation to the shareholders of the target company which allows them to make declarations of acceptance.

[196] Offers to purchase or exchange equity securities which are made in publicly accessible media (of any kind) are deemed to be a public offer governed by the Swiss takeover rules. However, for the purposes of delimiting the scope of application of the Swiss rules on takeovers, the function of the rules must be taken into account, which lies in the *protection of* those *holders of equity securities* who can only accept or reject an offer and who are not in a position to negotiate the terms of the purchase and/or exchange due to the size of the group of targeted shareholders. The TOB has ruled in the past that an offer to sixty-four to eighty-seven shareholders certainly qualifies as a public offer. However, it is quite possible that even a much smaller number of addressees will suffice for such qualification.

[197] By contrast, *successive purchases* of equity securities on or off a stock exchange without a public offer being made (creeping tender offers) are not considered to be public offers.

Partial Offer for Equity Securities

[198] The principle of *equal treatment* of shareholders requires that an offer must in principle cover all categories of listed equity securities, i.e., shares, profit-sharing certificates and participation certificates.

[199] *Partial* offers are admissible under the Swiss rules on takeovers if the following conditions are met: (i) the offer must include all categories of listed equity securities; (ii) a partial offer cannot include equity securities whose acquisition would trigger the obligation to make a mandatory offer (change of control offer); (iii) the offeror must satisfy the acceptance declarations on a pro-rata basis (i.e., proportionately) if the offeror receives declarations of acceptance that go beyond the partial offer.

Equity Securities, Participation Certificates, Profit-Sharing Certificates a Other Securities

[200] The Swiss takeover rules apply to offers for equity securities, i.e., shares, pa ticipation certificates and profit-sharing certificates as well as conversion a option rights relating to such equity securities, including convertible bonds. Offe for *debt securities* do not trigger the application of the Swiss takeover rules unle such securities are provided with conversion or option rights.

Merger Transactions and Buyback Programmes

[201] According to the practice of the TOB in connection with merger transa tions, the Swiss takeover rules only apply if the respective shareholders are giver choice in the process under consideration, i.e., if they may accept or refuse an off The takeover law thus becomes applicable if shareholders are called upon choose between different alternatives, e.g., to retain their equity securities or exchange them. Accordingly, a *merger* is not subject to the rules on takeovers if t exchange of equity securities is mandatory for the shareholders of the absorb company.

[202] According to the practice of the TOB, a public offer by a listed company f its own equity securities, including the announcement of such intention (buyba programmes) constitutes a public takeover offer. *Buyback programmes* are in pri ciple subject to the Swiss takeover rules, unless exempted relief is granted by t TOB.

2.7.2 Responsibilities of the Board of a Target Company

Duty of the Board to Submit a Report

[203] The board of directors of the target company is responsible for submittin *report to the holders of equity securities* setting out the board's opinion about the off The information in the report must be true and complete and the report must published either in the offer prospectus or separately.

[204] The report of the board must contain all information that is required for t recipients of the offer to be able to make an *informed decision*. The report, in partic lar, has to explain the effect of the offer on the offeree company and its shareho ers. In addition, the board is obliged to amend and re-publish the report in t event of significant developments.

[205] The board may include a recommendation to accept or reject the offer, b the board can also refrain from making a recommendation and enumerate t advantages and disadvantages of the offer instead. The TOB requires that t board's opinion is *based on the facts set out in the report*. This means in particular th if the recommendation of the board of directors of the offeree company is based the assessment of a third party (i.e., fairness opinion), the fairness opinion mu form an integral part of the report. It is common practice to obtain a fairness opinion, in particular as a measure for neutralising potential or current conflicts of interests of members of the board.

[206] If the target company intends to take *defensive measures* or has already taken such measures, the report of the board needs to indicate such as well and the report has to outline the intentions of each shareholder owning more than 3% of the voting rights, provided, however, that such intentions are known to the board.

Defensive Measures by the Target Company

[207] As soon as an offer is published, the board of the target company *is limited in taking defensive measures*. In particular, the board may not enter into any legal transactions which would have the effect of significantly altering the assets or liabilities of the target. The restriction lasts until the result of the offer is announced. This rule serves to eliminate the influence of conflicts of interest that (may) exist on the part of the board and also the management in the event of unfriendly takeover offers.

[208] If the target company considers taking defensive measures it has to *notify the TOB* about such measures. This is, in particular, to ensure that the TOB can intervene in due time before inadmissible defensive measures have an effect on a takeover offer.

[209] Defensive measures which the general meeting of shareholders decide to take are not subject to the restriction and may be implemented irrespective as to whether such a decision was adopted before or after the publication of the offer.

[210] The TOB interprets the term *'defensive measure'* broadly. It is sufficient that a measure is suitable for making a takeover more difficult or to prevent it. A respective intention of the board is not a prerequisite for a measure to be considered inadmissible by the TOB.

2.7.3 Voluntary Offers

[211] Voluntary offers are all offers that do not qualify as mandatory offers. The restrictions of the Swiss takeover rules for mandatory offers do not apply to *voluntary offers*.

[212] In particular, a voluntary offer can be limited to the number of securities which the offeror deems appropriate and the offeror can make partial offers. The *offeror is free* to determine the amount of the offer price as the minimum price rules do not in principle apply to voluntary offers. The voluntary offer may be subject to conditions.

[213] The offer can be in the form of a cash offer or an exchange offer. In principle, the offeror is in a position to offer cash, equity securities or a combination of both as consideration. A cash alternative is not a prerequisite for a voluntary exchange offer. However, if the price consists entirely or partially of securities, the offeror must offer the shareholders a complete cash payment (cash alternative) if it acquires equity securities of the target company for cash in the period between th publication of the offer and its settlement.

[214] As soon as a voluntary offer comprises equity securities whose acquisitio would trigger the obligation to make an offer (change of control offer), the volun tary offer must comply with certain provisions of the *mandatory offer*. The voluntar offer must in particular cover all listed equity securities of the target company an the price of the offer must comply with the provisions on mandatory offers.

2.7.4 Principle of Equal Treatment

[215] The Swiss takeover rules stipulate that the offeror must *treat* all holders c equity securities of the same class *equally*.

[216] The offer must cover *all categories* of listed equity securities of the target com pany. If the offer also extends to unlisted equity securities of the target company o to equity derivatives, the principle of equal treatment also applies to such secur ties. The offer must also extend to equity securities derived from equity derivative until the end of the extension period, but not necessarily to the equity derivative themselves.

[217] Thus, if a target company has listed bearer shares and participation certif cates while its registered shares are not listed, the offeror can only make its offer i respect of the bearer shares and participation certificates and would not have t include the registered shares in the offer. If the *registered shares* are neverthele included in the offer, the principles of equal treatment will also be applied to th registered shares. These rules also apply to mandatory offers.

Conditions

In General

[218] Voluntary offers (including offers that extend to equity securities, the acqu sition of which would trigger the obligation to make a mandatory offer) may be sub ject to certain conditions if they cumulatively meet the following four *prerequisites*

(1) Conditions are only permissible if the offeror has a *justified interest* and the conditions are connected with the offer.
(2) The condition must *not* be of a *potestative nature*, i.e., it must be outside th offeror's sphere of influence.
(3) According to the practice of the TOB, the condition must be *sufficiently pre cise* so that it is clear at the end of the offer period whether it has been me
(4) According to the practice of the TOB, the condition must *not be unfair*. I particular, a condition is considered to be unfair if its content is unlawful c if its occurrence presupposes that the target company behaves unlawfull or, for example, breaches a transaction agreement.

Conditions That Are Valid until the Completion of the Offer

[219] Conditions that are valid until the completion of the offer are subject to two additional prerequisites:

(1) the offeror must prove that it has an *overriding interest* in the condition; and
(2) the *TOB* must *approve* such conditions.

In accordance with the *practice* of the TOB it follows that (i) minimum acceptance conditions with regard to the success rate of the offer are only valid until the expiry of the offer period, (ii) conditions which require a resolution of the shareholders' meeting of the target company or an entry in the Commercial Register to occur (amendment of the articles of association or election to the board of directors) will be valid until their execution, (iii) conditions, with which the execution of the offer is to be guaranteed can apply in principle up to the execution, and (iv) conditions designed to exclude inadmissible defensive measures may, in principle, apply until execution while material adverse change conditions, on the other hand, apply in principle only until the expiry of the offer period.

2.7.5 Mandatory Offers

Duty to Make an Offer

[220] Under the Swiss takeover rules, a *mandatory offer* to acquire all listed equity securities of the target has to be made by anyone who directly, indirectly or acting in concert with third parties acquires equity securities which, added to the equity securities already owned, exceed the threshold of 33⅓% (or 49% if the target company implemented an opting up) of the voting rights of the target, irrespective as to whether the voting rights are exercisable or not. However, voting rights that are exclusively exercised at the shareholders' meeting based on power of attorney do not count towards the threshold for making a mandatory offer.

[221] The *purpose* of the obligation to make an offer is to protect the minority shareholders against a change of control and the legal and factual possibilities of a major or majority shareholder which may be abused to the detriment of the minority shareholders. Therefore, the Swiss rules on takeovers foresee an exit option at an appropriate price.

[222] A company may raise the *threshold* for mandatory offers to 49% of the voting rights by incorporating a respective clause into its articles of association (opting up). A company may also, prior to the listing of their equity securities on a stock exchange, incorporate a respective clause into its articles of association, stating that an offeror will not be bound by the obligation to make a public takeover offer (opting out).

[223] An acquisition as defined by the Swiss takeover rules and thus the *trigger* fo the obligation to make a mandatory offer is the time of the acquisition of owne ship. In other words, it is not the entering into an obligation to transfer the equi securities that is decisive, but the actual transfer of shares.

Rules on the Price of the Offer

[224] The *rules on the price* of an offer are very essential provisions of the regulatic of an offer and for the protection of minority shareholders.

[225] If a shareholder is under the obligation to make a mandatory offer, the pri offered must be at least as high as the higher of either (i) the stock exchange pri or (ii) the highest price that the offeror has paid for equity securities of the targ company in the preceding twelve months (price of the previous acquisition). Th rule ensures that the holder of equity securities can sell at least at the *market pri* prior to the change of control and, on the other hand, can participate in the pr mium paid as part of the acquisition.

Stock Exchange Price

[226] The *stock exchange price* corresponds to the volume-weighted average price the on-order-book trades of the last sixty trading days prior to publication of th offer or the preliminary notification, but adjusted to negate the effects of signi cant price influences triggered by special events, such as dividend distributions c capital transactions, which the exchange price is subject to during this period.

[227] If the listed equity securities are *not liquid* prior to disclosure of the offer c prior announcement, a company evaluation must be prepared by an audit firn The same applies for equity securities that are not listed.

[228] If the target company has issued *several classes* of equity securities, the rat between the offered prices for the different classes of equity securities must b appropriate.

Sale at a Premium

[229] Until 1 May 2013 and the respective revision of the Swiss takeover rules, a offeror was allowed to pay a *premium* for larger blocks of shares, whereby the mir mum price of an offer was not allowed to be 25% below the highest price paid b the offeror in the last twelve months prior to the publication of the offer. No pr mium can be paid since the revision of 1 May 2013, except where the target h implemented an opting out clause in its articles of association. In this case, the of eror is free to pay a premium before the announcement of an offer or prior to i publication.

[230] The *value of equity securities* offered for exchange will be determined in acco dance with the principles for determining the offer price.

Best Price Rule

[231] If the offeror acquires equity securities of the target company in the period running from the publication of the offer or the announcement of the offer until six months after the additional acceptance period at a price that exceeds the *offer price*, it must offer this price to all recipients of the offer (best price rule). The best price rule applies to mandatory offers as well as to voluntary offers and it also applies to the acquisition of participation derivatives and to offers relating to such instruments.

Conditions

[232] In the case of mandatory offers, conditions can only be included in the offer for *important reasons*. This also applies to voluntary offers if the offeror crosses the threshold value for the obligation to make a mandatory offer during the offer period because it buys equity shares outside the offer. In such case, any conditions that are inadmissible for mandatory offers have to be deleted from the voluntary offer.

2.7.6 Various Aspects of a Public Takeover

Exclusivity Agreement

[233] Exclusive agreements that only govern the duration of the negotiations before the publication of a pre-announcement or an offer are usually not problematic from the point of view of the Swiss takeover rules, since they do not apply after this period. The considerations under stock exchange law do not yet apply during this period and they only come into effect when a *pre-announcement* or an offer is published.

[234] *After the publication* of a pre-announcement or an offer, clauses are inadmissible that would oblige the target company to refrain from negotiating with a competing offeror or provide it with the same information that the target company has already provided to the previous offeror, as this would be contrary to the principle of equal treatment.

Break-Up Fees

[235] An agreement on break-up fees *obliges the target company to pay* a certain amount to an offeror in case its offer fails.

[236] The TOB has not, from the point of view of the Swiss takeover rules, objected to a break-up fee in a number of cases. The TOB considers the amount of the break-up fee to be decisive; this must not deter third parties from making an offer or restrict shareholders' freedom of choice. A break-up fee must therefore be *proportionate in its amount* and be based in particular on the costs incurred by the offeror as a result of the offer.

Tender Agreement

[237] The Swiss takeover rules *do not prohibit* the conclusion of a tender agreeme i.e., an agreement between the offeror and a shareholder to accept the offer befo the beginning of the offer period, and the tender agreement also does not cons tute a transaction outside the offer.

[238] According to prevailing doctrine, a tender agreement does not trigger t obligation to make a *mandatory offer*. If the shareholders confine themselves to co mitting to transfer their shares if the offer is made and if they otherwise have active role in relation to the offer, such an agreement is irrelevant under takeov law. However, if a tender agreement includes a duty for the shareholder to coop ate with the offeror, such may qualify as acting in concert and trigger respecti obligations.

Due Diligence

[239] In principle, the target company is under *no obligation* to permit a due di gence examination by the offeror(s) prior to or during an offer period. In additio the offeror may not make its offer subject to the condition that due diligence granted, as this would inadmissibly put the board of directors in a predicame The offeror further may not state a price in the pre-notification and combine tl with a general indication that this price will only be increased if a satisfactory d diligence has been carried out.

[240] On the other hand, the offeror is permitted to make a *reservation* in the p announcement to reduce the offer price should it make negative findings in a d diligence. However, the offeror may not rely on the fact that it will be able to ca out a due diligence at a later stage in the takeover process and that it will be able deduct the full amount equal to the negative findings resulting from the due di gence.

[241] Under certain circumstances, however, an *obligation* of the target company grant due diligence may actually arise. This is true in particular if the target co pany granted a due diligence to a competing offeror (results from the equal tre ment requirement under Swiss takeover rules).

Publicly Available Information on the Target Company

[242] Target companies listed on a stock exchange in Switzerland are subject to t *disclosure obligations* imposed by the regulations of the *respective stock exchange* whi set the minimum standard for the disclosure of information.

[243] However, listed companies may *voluntarily* disclose *more information* th required by the stock exchange regulations in order to close the information g between the listed company (target company) and the investors.

[244] Listed companies are *obliged* to publish the *following information* and invest can obtain the information they need to make an informed investment decisi under the principles as set out in the following:

(a) Ad hoc publicity
The target company listed on a stock exchange is obliged to publish potentially *price-sensitive* facts electronically by means of a media release (so-called ad hoc announcement).

(b) Annual report
The target company must prepare an annual report with *audited financial statements* in accordance with the applicable accounting standards (including a chapter on corporate governance), publish it together with the corresponding report of the audit company (auditor's certificate) and submit it to the stock exchange. A semi-annual report must also be published.

(c) Corporate calendar
The target company must further publish on its website a corporate calendar containing certain *important information* for market participants (e.g., the publication dates of the financial reports or the date of the next annual shareholders' meeting).

(d) Management transactions
The stock exchange must be notified of transactions in equity securities as well as conversion and purchase rights in respect of shares by members of the *board* of directors and the executive board of a listed company.

(e) Regular reporting obligations
Listed companies are further subject to regular reporting obligations in order to *maintain the listing* of their equity securities or other instruments.

Transaction Reporting

[245] From the date of publication of the offer until the end of the additional acceptance period, all parties to the proceedings must *notify the TOB* and the relevant disclosure office about (i) any transactions they have carried out involving equity securities of the target company or related participation derivatives and (ii) in the case of a public exchange offer: any transactions involving the securities offered in exchange and the related participation derivatives. This obligation to report also applies to anyone who directly or indirectly holds at least 3% of the voting rights in the target company or the company whose securities are being offered in exchange.

[246] Anyone who is *acting in concert* with the offeror or shareholders subject to the reporting rules is subject to the same reporting obligations.

Ad Hoc Publicity Duties During a Takeover Period

[247] Target *companies listed* on a stock exchange in Switzerland (SIX Swiss Exchange or BX Swiss) are subject to rules on ad hoc publicity which aim to ensure that all current and potential market participants have equal opportunity to access potential price-sensitive information (ad hoc publicity). This should ensure maximum transparency and equal treatment of market participants.

[248] However, ad hoc publicity is not a specific form of publicity duty under th Swiss takeover rules but regulates the information duties of listed companies *in gen eral*. During a public takeover offer, ad hoc publicity becomes even more importan for the target company since every single action of the target company may need t be published under the ad hoc publicity rules.

[249] Facts that must be published under the rules of ad hoc publicity must be *pub lished immediately* after their occurrence. The disclosure of price-sensitive informa tion may be deferred where a relevant fact is based on a plan or decision of th target company and the publication of that fact may potentially harm the interest of the target company. Such a deferral of ad hoc publicity is, however, only permis sible if the target company actually keeps the relevant fact or information secre Selective disclosure to individual market participants would violate the principle c equal treatment.

[250] Hence, the target company needs to publish *price-sensitive information* imme diately in the form of an ad hoc announcement in case such price-sensitive infor mation becomes known to only a few market participants due to a leak. It i advisable and common practice that the target company has an emergency com munication plan ready for such occurrences.

2.7.7 Disclosure Duties

[251] *Anyone* who directly or indirectly or acting in concert with third partie *acquires* or *disposes* of shares or acquisition or sale rights relating to shares of a com pany with its registered office in Switzerland whose equity securities are listed i whole or in part in Switzerland, or of a company with its registered office abroa whose equity securities are mainly listed in whole or in part in Switzerland, an thereby reaches, falls below or exceeds the *thresholds* of 3%, 5%, 10%, 15%, 20% 25%, $33\frac{1}{3}$%, 50% or $66\frac{2}{3}$% of the voting rights, whether exercisable or not, *mus notify* this to the company and the stock exchanges on which the equity securitie are listed.

[252] The objective is to ensure, in the interests of the investor, the *transparency* c the stock exchange, the functioning of trading and the equal treatment of marke participants.

2.7.8 General Comments on the Timetable

Period of the Offer

[253] The offer may be accepted only after a *cooling-off period* which is usually te trading days from publication of the offer prospectus in the newspapers. Th cooling-off period, however, may be lengthened or shortened by the TOB.

[254] The offer must then *remain open* for a period of at least twenty trading day this can, however, be shortened at the request of the offeror to ten trading days if (the offeror holds the majority of the voting rights in the target company before th publication of the offer; and (ii) the report of the board of directors of the target company is published in the offer prospectus.

[255] If the offer is successful, the offeror must grant a right of *retrospective acceptance* of the offer for a period of ten trading days from the date of publication of the final announcement of the interim result (additional acceptance period). The foregoing also applies to the unconditional offer.

Antitrust and Merger Control

[256] If under applicable antitrust law (or anti-cartel law) a takeover is only permissible if the relevant competition authorities agree (*see also* paragraph [364]), a corresponding offer must be made subject to the *condition* that these authorities grant the necessary authorisations.

[257] Where antitrust proceedings are more time consuming than the takeover process, the TOB may oblige the offeror to take over the validly offered equity securities of the target company independently of the pending antitrust proceedings and to find a solution which complies with antitrust law.

[258] According to its practice, the TOB *postpones the completion* of an offer for up to four months after expiry of the additional acceptance period (*see also* paragraph [365]). However, further extension due to still outstanding conditions is only permitted if the offeror can prove a special interest and credibly demonstrate that the outstanding conditions will be fulfilled within a relatively short period of time.

Impact of Competing Offers on the Timetable

[259] A '*competing offer*' is a tender offer that is published as a second offer in competition with an existing initial offer. The first offer is referred to as the 'previous offer'. The term 'competing offer' refers both to a new offer and to an existing offer that is being amended.

[260] The publication of a competing offer has various effects on the *timetable* of a public takeover transaction. First, the schedules of the two offers are automatically adjusted so that the offer periods expire simultaneously. If the competing offer expires after the previous offer, the latter will automatically be extended until the competing offer expires. The same applies vice versa.

[261] If a competing offer is made, the previous *offer can be amended* no later than the fifth trading day prior to its expiry. However, the previous and competing offer can be amended no later than the last trading day of the offer period (before the start of exchange trading) only with the prior consent of the TOB. The amended offer must remain open for ten trading days. This period may then only be extended with the prior consent of the TOB. However, the offer period of the other offer will again be automatically extended as well.

[262] If none of the offers is changed by the fifth trading day prior to the expiry of the extended offer period, the *bidding procedure* is completed and, in principle, none of the offerors may amend their offer anymore. However, if one of the offe ors acquires shares in the target company in violation of the best price rule after th expiry of the deadline to amend the offer, the TOB may reopen the (actually com pleted) bidding process for a further period of ten trading days, which in retur gives the competing offeror the opportunity to increase its offer price again. Th rule theoretically permits an infinite sequence of offers and counter-offers and, as result, may extend the bidding process which may have a negative impact on th target company and tie up resources for an excessively long period.

2.7.9 General Comments on Content of Documents

Duties of Auditors: Examination of the Offer Prospectus

[263] The auditor (securities traders and audit companies licensed to audit secur ties traders) are authorised to examine offers. Prior to the publication of the offe the auditor verifies whether the *offer prospectus* complies with the Swiss takeov rules as well as with any decision by the TOB in connection with the offer. It must i particular verify: (i) that the offer prospectus is complete and accurate, (ii) wheth the recipients of the offer have been treated equally, (iii) how the financing of th offer is done and whether funds are available, (iv) the availability of any securiti offered in exchange. In the upcoming Swiss Federal Act on Financial Servic (FinSA), the requirements and content of a prospectus are precisely regulate which must be examined and approved by a newly established auditing authorit

[264] The auditor has to prepare a *brief report*, which the offeror must publish i the offer prospectus.

Duties of Auditor after Publication of the Offer

[265] After publication of the offer, the *auditor* has to verify whether the provisio of the Swiss takeover rules, as well as the decisions of the TOB in connection wit the offer, have been complied with throughout the offer period. It has to in partic lar outline (i) the notifications of the transactions, (ii) the publication of interi and final results, (iii) the proper settlement of the offer, (iv) the compliance with th rules on voluntary exchange offers and the best price rule.

[266] The auditor has to submit a *final report* to the TOB, specifying the principl on which it has based its examination.

2.7.10 Withdrawal of the Offer

[267] The offeror is *not allowed* to revoke the offer after publication of the off prospectus or the pre-announcement, but remains bound to its offer even in th event of changes to the market situation or the target company. However, the of eror may at least make its offer subject to conditions which, in the event of corr sponding changes, may lead to the offer not materialising.

[268] Since this binding effect of the offer is of *compelling* nature, the offeror is not allowed to provide for the possibility of revocation in the offer prospectus.

2.7.11 Settlement of the Offer

[269] Usually, the offer must be settled no later than ten trading days after the end of the additional *acceptance period*. If the offer remains subject to conditions, settlement may be postponed with the prior consent of the TOB. The time of settlement must be indicated in the offer prospectus.

2.7.12 Rules on Squeeze-Out of Minority Shareholders

[270] If the offeror after successful completion of a public offer holds more than 98% of the voting rights of the target company, it may submit to the court (*see* paragraph [387]) a request for *cancellation* under the stock exchange law of these shares against payment of the offer price and to forcibly exclude these remaining holders of equity securities (public shareholders) who still hold shares in the target company (squeeze out).

[271] If the *court* declares the remaining 2% of the shares in the target company to be cancelled, the holders of these remaining shares will lose their position as shareholders in the target company upon the decision taking legal effect and will instead acquire a claim to payment of the offer price.

2.7.13 Violation of the Swiss Takeover Rules

Breach of Notification Duties

[272] A fine not exceeding CHF10 m will be imposed on any person who *wilfully* (i) violates the *disclosing duties* or (ii) as the owner of a qualified participation in a target company fails to disclose the acquisition or sale of equity securities of that company. If a violation is committed through negligence, the fine will not exceed CHF100 000.

Breach of the Duty to Make an Offer

[273] A fine of up to CHF10 m will be imposed on anyone who *deliberately* fails to comply with a legally binding obligation to submit an *offer*.

[274] Further, if there are sufficient indications that a person has not met the duty to make an offer, the TOB may take the following *measures* until the duty to make an offer has been clarified or, as appropriate, the duty to make an offer has been fulfilled:

(a) *Suspend* the voting rights and associated rights of this person; and
(b) *Prohibit* this person from acquiring further shares or acquisition or disposal rights relating to shares of the target company, be it directly, indirectly or acting in concert with third parties.

Breach of Duties by the Target Company

[275] A fine not exceeding CHF500 000 will be imposed on any person who *u fully* (i) fails to submit the *mandatory report* to the holders of equity securities setti out their position in relation to the offer or fails to publish such a report or (includes untrue or incomplete information in such a report. If a violation is co mitted through negligence, the fine will not exceed CHF150 000.

2.8 IP and Other Relevant Laws

(by Adrian Bieri)

2.8.1 IP Law

Registration and Protection of IP Rights in Switzerland

[276] In Switzerland, registrable IP includes patents, trademarks, designs, topo raphies and some specific indications of source while *copyrights* (rights of authc ship) *are not registrable* since there is no copyright registration system under Sw copyright law.

[277] A *patent* is an exclusive right granted for the protection of new inventio (related to products or processes) during a limited period of up to twenty years. return for this limited monopoly, the owner of a patent must disclose the inventi to the public in the patent application. For obtaining patent protection, a pate application must be filed, since registration is a requirement for obtaining pate protection.

[278] A *trademark* is a sign (any word, name, symbol or device, or any combinati thereof) that distinguishes the goods or services of one company from those of ot ers. Trademarks duly registered in the Swiss trademark register offer protection f ten years, but trademark protection can be renewed repeatedly for periods of t years.

[279] A *design* is a creation of products or parts thereof which is especially char terised by the arrangement of lines, surfaces, contours or colour, or by the mater used. The Swiss Design Act thereby provides protection for all externally perce tible features of a product's appearance without focussing on its intended purpo Designs duly registered in the Swiss design register offer protection for five ye and can be renewed by four further protective terms of five years each, up tc maximum duration of twenty-five years.

[280] *Copyright* protects creations of literature and art that have a unique charact This includes literature, music, pictures, sculptures, films, operas, ballets, choreo raphies and pantomimes. Swiss copyright law not only offers protection for su creations in the traditional field of art and culture but creations in the field industry and trade, such as designs of a technical kind and advertising diagrams well as scientific texts or computer programs can also benefit from trademark protection. Copyright protection applies as soon as a work is created and ends seventy years (in case of computer programs fifty years) after the death of the author.

[281] Applications for the registration of registrable IP rights must be filed with the *Swiss Federal Institute of Intellectual Property* in Bern.

Typical Areas of Due Diligence Undertaken with Respect to IP Assets in Switzerland

[282] In general terms, due diligence with respect to IP assets aims at revealing the value of the target company's intangible assets by *analysing the relevance of intellectual property* for the valuation of its business. The scope and depth of due diligence depend on the relevance of IP for the valuation of the target company's business and, hence, its impact on the value of the transaction.

[283] Typical areas of due diligence undertaken in Switzerland include the *identification of business-related intellectual property* of the target company and a review of whether the company actually owns the IP rights used for its business. If third parties or shareholders own the IP rights used by the target company, due diligence includes an analysis of whether the target company has concluded sufficient licence agreements for the continued use of such intangible assets.

[284] The due diligence undertaken with regard to ownership includes the assessment whether the IP *registrations are up to date*, whether a clear and *complete chain of title* can be identified, and whether there are *security interests or liens* created over the IP. The key focus of due diligence undertaken with respect to IP assets is to ensure the title to and scope of protection of the IP assets. The buyer has to analyse whether IP rights are owned by the target company and are validly registered in the countries where the company is conducting business.

[285] Further areas of due diligence include the review of any IP-related *litigation* by and against the target company. The aim is to verify whether any third party is, or is suspected to be, infringing the target company's IP rights and whether the target company is infringing a third party's IP rights (freedom to operate).

[286] The sale of a company by way of a *share deal* (*see* paragraphs [66] et seq.) entails the transfer of the company as a whole, with all assets and liabilities – which means that assets and liabilities do not have to be transferred individually. Conversely, this also means that any liability in the company must be detected and assessed, because it will have a negative impact on the target – and, thus, also on the value of the technology. Accordingly, in transactions in the legal form of a share deal, comprehensive due diligence with respect to all of the company's IP must be undertaken.

[287] In an *asset deal* (*see* paragraphs [83] et seq.), to the contrary, the buyer acquires specific assets (and, if so agreed, liabilities) from the target company, often in a series of individual, although simultaneous and connected transactions. The due diligence of IP rights undertaken for transactions in the legal form of an asset deal is, therefore, limited to the IP asset(s) which the buyer intends to acquire.

[288] With regard to non-registered (whether non-registrable or not) *technica know-how, data and secrets*, key due diligence areas will typically include employmen and employees as well as advisors (contracts, confidentiality obligations and prohi bition on exploitation, transfer of IP rights related to work results), organisatio (measures in place to preserve the confidentiality of know-how and data) and cus tomers (customer base and behaviour, customer contracts).

2.8.2 Agency and Distribution Law

General Remarks

[289] According to the legal definition under the CO, an *agent* is 'a person wh undertakes to act on a continuous basis as an intermediary for one or more princi pals in facilitating or concluding transactions on their behalf and for their accoun without entering into an employment relationship with them'. The most importan differentiating criterion compared to other forms of distribution is ultimately tha the agent typically sells the principal's goods and services for the principal' account and at the principal's economic risk. The agency relationship, in genera is governed by Articles 418a et seq. CO.

[290] '*Distributor*' means an independent trader, dealing in their own name and fo their own account in goods or services produced by a third party, the 'supplier' Therefore and in contrast to an agent, the distributor sells the products at thei own economic risk. Since the CO provides no specific regulation for distributio agreements, it is recommended that the parties to a distribution agreement defin their obligations and the consequences of performance in detail. Switzerland gen erally takes a liberal view on distribution relationships, and distribution agree ments are a common and important form for Swiss firms to organise th distribution of their goods and services in the form of indirect sales systems wit third parties.

Agent's Claim to Compensation for Clientele

[291] In the event that the agent's activities have resulted in a substantial expan sion of the principal's clientele and considerable benefits accrue even after the en of the agency relationship to the principal from its business relations with client acquired by the agent, the agent has a claim for *adequate compensation* in the event c termination of the agency agreement, provided that this is not inequitable).

[292] As this statutory provision governing the compensation of clientele (Articl 418u CO) is *mandatory*, it may not be validly waived before the end of the agenc agreement or before such claim has arisen. This compensation is not considered t be additional remuneration for services provided by the agent, but rather as com pensation for an added value generated for the principal based on investment made by the agent during the agency relationship.

[293] Clientele means not just an address list, but a real customer base, allowing the agent's replacement to continue the agent's activities. An *expansion of the principal's clientele* is considered *substantial* if it has a certain economic significance. In the past, the expansion of a customer base from 85 to 123 in 2 years and the acquisition of 200 clients in 14 years have been qualified as economically significant by Swiss courts. The expansion of the principal's client base must have its cause in the activities of the agent.

[294] The substantial expansion of the client base must bring a *considerable benefit to the principal*. Only if there is a high probability of the clientele remaining loyal to the principal, the expansion will be considered beneficial for the principal.

[295] This condition may be fulfilled under the following circumstances:

- if the agent is under a contractual obligation *to hand over its customer list* to the supplier as this enables the principal, upon the termination of the agency agreement, to take over the client base acquired by the agent; and/or
- if products with a *strong brand* are the subject of the agency agreement since clients generally remain loyal to the brand (and not to the agent). This is particularly true with regard to premium brands.

[296] Lastly, the compensation payment may *not* be *inequitable*, which would be the case, for example, if the term of the agency agreement and the agent's profits made during such term would be disproportionate against an additional compensation. The courts have a wide range of discretion not only to lower its amount but also to completely deny compensation on clientele to the agent if such a compensation appears inequitable.

[297] The amount of such claim may not exceed the *agent's net annual earnings* from the agency relationship, calculated as the *average* for the last five years or, where shorter, the average over the entire duration of the contract.

[298] No claim to compensation for clientele exists where the agency relationship was terminated for a reason attributable to the agent.

Distributor's Claim to Compensation for Clientele

[299] The answer to the question of whether or not a distributor may claim compensation for clientele in the event of the termination of a distribution agreement was controversial until a landmark decision by the SFSC in the year 2008, which has been recently backed up by another similar decision by the SFSC. According to current court practice, which has been both supported and criticised by Swiss legal doctrine, the SFSC *applies Article 418u paragraph 1 CO*, which governs the agent's claim to compensation for clientele, *mutatis mutandis* under distribution agreements, provided that *certain conditions* are fulfilled.

[300] The following requirements must be fulfilled for a distributor to have a (mandatory) claim to compensation for clientele against a supplier: (i) the requirements for an analogous application of Article 418u paragraph 1 CO, due to an *agent-like position* of the distributor, must be fulfilled and (ii) in case such requir- ments for an analogous application are fulfilled, the *conditions set forth in Artic 418u paragraph 1 CO*, must also be fulfilled.

[301] According to the SFSC's court practice, an analogous application of Artic 418u paragraph 1 CO is justified if (i) the *supplier retains a very extensive right of co- trol against the distributor* and (ii) the *supplier obliges the distributor to integrate into th supplier's sales organisation* so that the distributor finds itself in an agent-like positio and only has limited economic autonomy.

[302] *Elements* that could *evidence* an agent-like position may include the followin

- the supplier's right to approve new points of sale proposed by the distributo
- the distributor's obligation to acquire an annual minimum quantity of th products;
- the supplier's right to unilaterally change the prices or terms of delivery fo the products;
- the supplier's right to cease production or marketing of a product at an time;
- the distributor's obligation to carry minimum stock of the product;
- the distributor's obligation for monthly submission of various reports an lists concerning turnover and competitors' activities to the supplier;
- the distributor's obligation to disclose its books and directories;
- the distributor's obligation to periodically notify the supplier of the nam and addresses of customers;
- the distributed product has a strong brand name;
- the distributor is not allowed to continue to sell the products after the end the distribution agreement.

The more of the above elements apply, the higher the likelihood that Artic 418u paragraph 1 CO may be applied analogously to a distribution agreement.

[303] As already mentioned before, if the requirements for an analogous applic- tion of Article 418u paragraph 1 CO are fulfilled, the conditions pursuant Article 418u paragraph 1 CO itself must also be fulfilled. Pursuant to Article 418 paragraph 1 CO, the *following requirements must be fulfilled for a claim* on compens- tion for clientele:

(a) substantial expansion of the supplier's clientele base by the distributor;
(b) the supplier benefits from the clientele base established or expanded by th distributor upon the termination of the distribution agreement; and
(c) the compensation must not be inequitable.

[304] With respect to the calculation of the claim on compensation for clientel the SFSC referred, in general terms, to Article 418u paragraph 1 CO governing a agent's right to compensation for clientele. According to the said article, a claim fo compensation may not exceed an agent's *net earnings for one year* under the contra tual relationship, based on the *average* for the last five years.

2.8.3 Anti-bribery and Anti-corruption Laws

Prohibition of Bribery under the PC and the Unfair Competition Act

[305] Generally, the PC prohibits *active and passive bribery of Swiss officials* (Article 322*ter* and 322*quarter*), namely the offering, promising or giving (and, on the other hand, soliciting, receiving a promise of, or accepting) of an undue advantage to a member of a judicial or other authority, a public official, an officially appointed expert, translator or interpreter, an arbitrator, or a member of the armed forces an undue advantage, or offers, promises or gives such an advantage to a third party in order to cause the public official to carry out or to fail to carry out an act in connection with their official activity which is contrary to their duty or dependent on their discretion.

[306] Until 1 July 2016, private commercial bribery used to be prosecuted only in case of a restriction of competition and only upon complaint by a competitor, under the Unfair Competition Act.

[307] The PC was amended and, since 1 July 2016, now also prohibits *private bribery*. Under Article 322*octies* (private active bribery) and Article 322*novies* (private passive bribery), private bribery is prosecuted ex officio. In minor cases, it is prosecuted upon complaint.

[308] Private active bribery, under the PC, is described as follows: 'Any person who offers, promises or gives an employee, partner, agent or any other auxiliary of a third party in the private sector an undue advantage for that person or a third party in order that the person carries out or fails to carry out an act in connection with their official activities which is contrary to their duties or dependent on their discretion is liable to a custodial sentence not exceeding three years or to a monetary penalty.'

[309] *Private passive bribery* under the PC is the act by any person who as an employee, partner, agent or any other auxiliary of a third party in the private sector demands, secures the promise of, or accepts an undue advantage.

Enforcement of the Laws and Evolution

[310] Although laws are generally well enforced, only some few cases of corruption are reported.

[311] Moreover, since active and passive bribery in the private sector are considered misdemeanours, acts of money laundering for the proceeds of private corruption are not prosecuted. *Money laundering* in Switzerland is, indeed, only prosecuted for the proceeds of a felony (sentence of five years or more).

[312] Scrutiny has become stronger, in particular, due to media reports. In recent years, Swiss enforcement authorities have investigated many Swiss companies and foreign companies with operations in Switzerland for alleged corruption and suspicious activity.

Effect of the 'Long Reach' of the US Foreign Corrupt Practices Act and the UK Bribery Act M&A Activity in Switzerland

[313] Because of the extraterritorial reach of these laws, cross-border transacti agreements usually contain *anti-corruption warranty clauses* which state, among oth things, that the seller did not violate or breach any provisions of the United Stat Foreign Corrupt Practices Act (FCPA), the United Kingdom Bribery Act (UK-B or any similar national or local anti-bribery or anti-corruption laws or regulatio

[314] Such *representations* in M&A agreements make it possible for buyers to ensu that they do not take over the consequences of breaches of foreign acts, especially the target company operates in the US or the UK.

2.8.4 Anti-money Laundering Regulations

[315] *Article 305 PC* provides for the prosecution of any person who carries out act that is aimed at frustrating the identification of the origin, the tracing or t forfeiture of assets which they know or must assume to originate from a felony aggravated tax misdemeanour.

[316] Secondly, the *Swiss Anti-Money Laundering Act (AMLA)*, along with its or nance which applies to financial intermediaries, regulates the combating of mon laundering (as defined by Article 305b PC), the combating of terrorist financing (defined by Article 260*quinquies* paragraph 1 PC) and the due diligence required financial transactions.

2.8.5 Environmental and Product Safety Laws

[317] Environmental and product safety laws may also have to be considered.

[318] A wide range of federal statutes *protect natural resources*. The main ones a the Federal Environmental Protection Act, the Federal Water Protection Act, t Federal Act on the Protection of Nature and Cultural Heritage, the Federal For Act, the Federal Agriculture Act and the Federal Act on Non-Human Gene Tec nology.

[319] The Product Safety Act governs the *safety of products* sold on the Swiss mark at a product level.

[320] Since the Act came into force on 1 July 2010, Switzerland has establish general requirements that subsidiarily apply to a selection of products. The Pro uct Safety Act aligned Switzerland's product safety regulations with the EU Produ Safety Directive (2001/95/EEC). Before the Act came into force, only the safety technical equipment and devices was regulated by a product-overarching a whereas the safety of all other products was governed by sectoral law, if at all.

2.9 Due Diligence

(by Thomas Peter)

2.9.1 General Comments

[321] Allowing potential buyers to perform a due diligence investigation is common in Switzerland for the contemplated purchase of closely held business enterprises. A satisfactory buy-side due diligence is not only in the interests of a buyer intending to mitigate risks but is also in the best interests of the seller as it may have a direct impact on the purchase price the buyer is prepared to pay.

[322] Accordingly, a seller will want to present the target company and/or its business in the most favourable light, and a seller will be well advised to invest a reasonable amount of effort and care in the preparation of the due diligence process. A carefully prepared, well-organised and substantially complete data room has a potentially *trust-building effect* on a buyer as it leaves the impression of a well-organised business. On the other hand, disorganised and incomplete data rooms raise a lot of questions, doubt and scepticism for a buyer and its professional advisors, which will result in a higher demand for further representations and warranties or indemnifications in the transaction agreement.

[323] Today, the disclosure of data is typically granted through *virtual data rooms* that allow a potential buyer to review all disclosed documents until signing or abortion of the transaction. It goes without saying that the disclosure of the relevant documents in the data room is subject to strict confidentiality obligations of the buyer and its advisors, which have to be accepted and confirmed upon login to the virtual data room. The constant availability of the online data room throughout the entire transaction process allows the buyer's advisors to limit their due diligence report on 'identified issues only' (rather than having to summarise the entire content of the data room for the benefit of the buyer who did not have the opportunity to review an entire physical data room).

[324] A due diligence investigation typically includes corporate, commercial, financial, employment and tax matters. Depending on the specific business and the assets of the target company, other issues such as IP or real estate matters may also be crucial. A careful buyer will *analyse* the business of the target before starting the due diligence process in order to identify its *value drivers* as well as specific *risks* related thereto.

[325] For example, real estate owned by a company typically represents a significant portion of such company's assets. It is, therefore, common to request the disclosure of relevant extracts from the land register evidencing not only the legal title to the land but also listing registered third party rights with regard to such property that may have an impact on its legal value. With regard to environmental matters, a buyer will want to check whether the real estate is registered as a contaminated site in the respective state register of contaminated sites, bearing in mind that any non-registration of the property in the register does not prove that it is not contaminated. However, an additional environmental audit would only seem reasonable if it were based on specific additional facts (such as the business activity conducted on the site).

[326] When disclosing business information to a buyer, a seller will have to ensure compliance with all laws imposing *confidentiality* obligations on the seller or the target company. In addition to *data protection* issues relating to employees, this includes, for example, compliance with Swiss *banking secrecy* in the event of the acquisition of a bank or (parts of) its business.

2.9.2 Critical Issues

[327] In addition to business- or asset-specific matters, a legal due diligence will in any event have to ensure that the buyer validly acquires full title to the shares or assets subject to the relevant purchase agreement. Typically, these matters are covered by the so-called fundamental representations pursuant to the transaction agreement. The fundamental importance of these issues obviously arises because if a relating risk materialises, damages may not offer a suitable remedy for a buyer.

[328] For example, if a buyer pays a full purchase price for shares which later turn out to be invalid or validly owned by a third party, the only appropriate remedy would be the rescission of the agreement in its entirety – a remedy that is usually excluded by the transaction agreement. In share deals governed by Swiss law, it is therefore of the utmost importance to verify that all shares subject to the relevant transaction are, directly or indirectly, *validly transferred* to the buyer at closing. Typical flaws would be that share certificates were not duly issued (because they were issued before the respective shares were registered in the Commercial Register) or because registered shares were not duly assigned to one of the previous shareholders in writing. Fundamental flaws in the title to shares or assets of this kind would ideally already be identified by the seller's counsels when preparing the data room (seller's due diligence) as, again, the identification of such fundamental issues in buyer's due diligence bears a risk of destroying a buyer's trust in the target company and the conduct of its business in general.

2.9.3 The Relationship Between the Due Diligence and Representations, Warranties and Indemnities

[329] In Switzerland, purchase agreements are typically based on the principle of *'general disclosure'*. This means that all matters and facts that were disclosed in the due diligence process (particularly in the data room as well as certain other documents or sources of information to be agreed upon) are regarded as known to the buyer and therefore excluded from the scope of the representations and warranties. Usually, the parties agree that in order to validly exclude the seller's liability such disclosure must have been 'fairly' made, meaning '[...] the disclosure of a fact, matter or circumstance in the disclosed documents [or otherwise] in a manner that enabled the buyer [or its advisors] [acting diligently] to identify [and assess the impact of] such fact, matter or circumstance [upon first reading of the document] [...]'.

[330] As a result, if a specific issue is identified during the due diligence process, the respective risk is not sufficiently covered from a buyer's perspective if a respective representation or warranty is included in the transaction agreement. Rather, by requesting such a representation or warranty, the buyer proves and admits that the underlying risk has been fairly disclosed which leads to an exclusion of the seller's liability for a breach of representations or warranties.

[331] Accordingly, matters identified in the course of a due diligence investigation will have to be covered by *specific indemnities* that constitute obligations of the seller to indemnify the buyer from losses suffered from the issue at hand, independently of whether or not such issue also qualifies as a breach of a representation or warranty (*see also* paragraphs [373] et seq.). Alternatively, the parties may, of course, always agree to cover a specific risk by a reduction of the purchase price.

2.10 Dispute Resolution and Enforcement

(by Kurt Blickenstorfer)

2.10.1 Dispute Resolution in General

[332] Switzerland is a civil law jurisdiction where case law is of less importance than in common law jurisdictions, since the primary sources of legal authority are written codes and statutes. There are no jury courts. Civil procedure before *courts* is generally governed by the Swiss Code of Civil Procedure (SCCP). In cross-border matters, especially with the EU, the Lugano Convention on Jurisdiction and the Recognition and Enforcement of Judgments in Civil and Commercial Matters (LugConv) must be observed in addition to the Swiss Federal Act on Private International Law (PILA), which is applicable to all international issues related to the conflict of private laws in Switzerland. It is to be noted that that the LugConv is no longer applicable to matters with the United Kingdom since Brexit.

[333] *Recovery of damages* is limited to the amount actually suffered; punitive damages are typically not available under Swiss law, but judgments that award sums of money usually include a statutory interest rate of 5%. Furthermore, the surrender of unlawfully earned profits can be found by courts. However, class actions are not possible and are unlikely to clear the hurdle of parliamentary discussion (yet)in the legislative process.

[334] *Resolutions* passed by the *general meeting* which violate the law or the articles of association may be challenged by bringing an action against the company before the court. Resolutions of the board of directors cannot be challenged in court.

[335] *Arbitration* is the only alternative to court litigation through which it is possible to achieve a final, binding and enforceable resolution of a dispute. Due to the liberal approach of the Swiss legal system towards arbitration and based on its political stability and neutrality, Switzerland has always played an important role i international arbitration. Zurich, Geneva and Basel are important arbitration ce tres for commercial disputes, while Lausanne is preferred for sports arbitration.

[336] For the amicable resolution of commercial disputes, *mediation* has becom quite popular. Generally speaking, mediation is a non-judicial method of confli resolution in which an impartial third party seeks to help resolve a dispute by faci tating settlement negotiations.

2.10.2 State Courts

Role of the Courts

[337] For *civil claims* the Swiss court system basically consists of *three instances*: at th cantonal level, the Courts of First Instance (mostly called District Courts) and on Court of Second Instance per canton (usually a Court of Appeal), and at the feder level, the Third and Final Instance, the SFSC. As a rule (with several exceptions the parties are required to participate in conciliation proceedings before an actio can be filed with a court. At a hearing, a conciliation judge tries to identify a settl ment that is satisfactory to both parties.

[338] However, the cantons are free to have specialised courts; in four canto (Zurich, Bern, St. Gallen and Aargau), *Commercial Courts* judge commercial disput (in particular those between companies) as the sole cantonal instance and the judgment can only be appealed to the SFSC. Prior to an action brought before Commercial Court, there still are no conciliation proceedings, but a change in th law under discussion is to allow this in the future. Furthermore, the Commerci Court itself usually holds settlement meetings with the parties.

[339] Often, the *parties agree* on a court to have *exclusive jurisdiction* over an existin or future pecuniary dispute arising from a particular legal relationship. The desi nated Swiss court must honour an exclusive jurisdiction clause, unless (a) anoth court has imperative jurisdiction over the subject matter of the case, (b) none of th parties is domiciled in a LugConv country, and (c) Swiss law is not applicable base on the merits of the case. In any event, the jurisdiction of an elected court arisin from a contractual clause conferring jurisdiction or from a provision of law may b contested.

[340] The Swiss constitution guarantees the *independence of judges and courts* b separation of powers. Cantonal and federal acts ensure with organisational an procedural provisions the independence of judges and courts from parties of a la suit. Based on personality, expertise, backbone, experience of life, and comm sense, judges are elected either by the public entitled to vote (very often for th Courts of First Instance) or appointed by a parliament (for instance, some courts appeal, Commercial Courts, and the SFSC). Most judges belong to a political part which supports their election. Such political influence very often is subject debate. Nevertheless, in various cases, judges have consistently found decisio against the ideas of their political party. And it can happen, albeit seldom, that judge fails in a re-election. Generally speaking, Swiss judges are independent, neutral and competent.

Court Proceedings

Trials

[341] Before a court, the parties must *present the facts*, typically in two written pleadings each, one after the other. Together with their pleadings, the parties must also file documentary evidence and offer any other *evidence permissible* under the SCCP on which they rely. The following types of evidence from the party bearing the burden of proof are admissible: documents, witness testimonies, expert opinions, written statements, inspections, and party assertions and testimonies. In summary proceedings, the parties are limited to evidence that can immediately be submitted to the judge, such as documents or written party statements. The SCCP does not provide for a pre-trial discovery phase. However, in specific circumstances, taking evidence as a precautionary measure is possible before the action is filed. During the trial, the parties may request a specific document that is in the possession of the opposing party or a third party.

[342] It should be noted that the parties are not required by law to present *legal arguments*, as it is presumed that the courts know the law. However, statutes of limitation are a matter of substantive civil law and are only considered by the court if invoked by a party.

[343] A defendant can file an application for a *third-party complaint* when filing the statement of defence. If the court admits this complaint and the third party decides against taking part in the trial, the third party is later barred from invoking certain defence when sued by the defendant in a recourse action.

[344] During the trial, the court can call the parties for *hearings*, mainly to facilitate a settlement. In such meetings, the judge may provide an opinion on legal issues and make the parties aware of the difficulty of proving crucial disputed facts.

[345] The trial ends with the issuance of the *judgment*. Courts may also render an interim decision (usually about the jurisdiction of the court) or a partial decision (specific kind of final decision with regard to only one part of the claim).

Interim Remedies

[346] Conservatory measures are intended *to secure the enforceability of a future judgment*. In cases of exceptional urgency, interim measures may be granted in ex parte proceedings.

[347] A motion for a *preliminary injunction* will be granted only if the application can show that the applicant is likely to prevail on the merits in the subsequent or a pending court case and that, in the absence of the requested injunction, the applicant will suffer irreparable harm. A possible measure is an order prohibiting the disposal of a business that is the subject of dispute.

[348] *Interim measures* may be sought in order to preserve the position of a pa until the dispute is resolved. The applicant must provide prima facie evidence th their right either was or likely will be violated and that this violation threatens cause harm that cannot easily be repaired. The court can order measures to reg late ongoing relationships or measures to require or prohibit certain actions. Al available are measures to preserve evidence that might otherwise be destroyed hidden.

[349] With such remedies, *restrictive covenants* given in an agreement (e.g., comp ing restrictions of the vendor towards the business sold) can be immediately a preliminary enforced during or even before a trial (*see also* paragraphs [370] a [373] et seq.).

[350] A creditor can secure the enforcement of a monetary claim by seeking *attac ment* of the debtor's assets. The creditor must prove, prima facie, the claim, t assets' location in Switzerland and the statutory ground for the attachment (f instance, the debtor's attempt to conceal assets, or a sufficient connection of t claim to Switzerland if the debtor's domicile is abroad). Often, the judge requi the applicant to post a bond for covering possible damages.

[351] If a person has reason to believe that they will receive a court order passed parte, such as a provisional order, a freezing order or an enforcement order und the LugConv, they can file *a preventive statement of defence* with the respective cou This statement must be renewed every six months and will only be brought to t attention of the opposing party after the latter has filed the anticipated request f interim measures.

Appeals

[352] Appeals must be lodged within a fixed deadline of thirty days or, in partic lar matters, of just ten days. In principle, it is possible *to challenge* the findings fact, the exercise of judicial discretion and the application of the law, but the parti must not make new allegations or raise new defences, except under very limit conditions. Decisions of a Commercial Court or a cantonal upper court can be ch lenged with an appeal to the SFSC if the amount in dispute is more than CHF 000, or if a legal question of fundamental importance is at stake. Although appeal, generally, does not have suspensive effect, the appellate court may, up motion, suspend the enforceability of the contested decision.

[353] Courts do not tend to favour domestic residents and companies over fo eigners, or individuals over businesses. Such preference would cause a complaint discrimination and a judgment based on discrimination could be challeng before the higher instance.

Duration and Cost

[354] On average, litigation before the first instance lasts between *one and th years*; before a Commercial Court it can last much longer if no settlement is reach during one of the settlement meetings. The duration before the second instance and then before the SFSC is generally shorter.

[355] *Court fees* are calculated on the basis of cantonal statutory rules and depend on the value in dispute. *Attorneys' fees* can be freely arranged between lawyers and their clients, usually at hourly rates. While contingency fees are not permitted, conditional fee arrangements providing for a base fee of a reasonable income and, in case of success, a bonus, which may not be higher than the base fee, are allowed. The party that is successful in court may recover costs from the opponent; however, attorneys' fees are usually not fully recoverable. A small number of third-party funding providers have established themselves in Switzerland. These request a share of the amount awarded in the judgment or in a settlement. In addition, legal expenses insurance has become a popular way to cover litigation costs, particularly for smaller disputes.

2.10.3 Alternative Dispute Resolution

Arbitration

[356] The parties frequently agree to submit their disputes to an arbitral tribunal, either ad hoc or under the rules of an institution. In Switzerland, a distinction is made between domestic and international arbitration. *International arbitration*, i.e., an arbitration where at least one of the parties has its domicile outside Switzerland when concluding the arbitration agreement, is governed by the PILA and is usually open to any pecuniary dispute. In contrast, *domestic arbitration* where all parties concerned are residents in Switzerland handles all claims a party may freely dispose of; it is governed by the SCCP. The parties, however, are free to agree in writing to opt out of or into the PILA or the SCCP.

[357] Very often in contractual arbitration clauses, reference is made to the arbitration rules of one of the arbitration organisations, such as the *Swiss Arbitration Centre Ltd.* with its Swiss Rules of International Arbitration or the *International Chamber of Commerce (ICC)* with its ICC Rules of Arbitration. Needless to say, United Nations Commission on International Trade Law (UNCITRAL) rules are also often chosen. Swiss courts may assist with the constitution of an arbitral tribunal, particularly with the appointment, removal or replacement of arbitrators.

[358] An international arbitral tribunal has the power to grant *interim measures*. And, if such provisional or protective measures are not observed by the relevant party, the arbitral tribunal can seek assistance from a court to enforce the appropriate order. *Provisional measures* may be granted by the arbitral tribunal or by a court upon application by a party. Swiss courts will also assist with the taking of evidence, among other things.

[359] Both domestic and international arbitration awards can only be *appealed* before the SFSC, unless, in the case of domestic arbitration, the parties have agreed to the jurisdiction of the upper court in the canton where the arbitration proceedings are held. The challenge of an international award is limited to Swiss public policy and certain essential procedural rights, while domestic awards can also be contested on the grounds of arbitrariness.

[360] *Costs* will be quite high, especially for smaller disputes, if the arbitral tribunal must consist of three arbitrators. Usually, the fee for the arbitral tribunal must be paid equally by the parties in advance, and if the defendant fails to pay, the plaintiff is required to provide the advance for both parties. Compared to state courts, however, arbitration proceedings are *much faster* once the arbitral tribunal has been constituted.

Mediation

[361] Because of its speed and efficiency, the cost of mediation is only a fraction of the cost of court proceedings or arbitration. Sometimes, the parties can find creative solutions for satisfying their various interests. The mediation process attempts to preserve the relationship between the parties that are in conflict and often helps to maintain ongoing relationships. The mediator does not have the authority to impose a binding solution on the parties. However, settlements reached through mediation are considered to be extrajudicial settlement agreements with the binding effect of an ordinary contract.

[362] The Swiss Arbitration Centre Ltd. has adopted the *Swiss Rules of Mediation* that includes a code of conduct for mediators. The ICC also has its own mediation rules. Other important institutions for mediation are the Swiss Chamber of Commercial Mediation (SCCM), the Swiss Federation of Mediation Associations (SDM-FSM) and the Swiss Bar Association (SAV-FSA).

Others

[363] Another possibility of alternative dispute resolution available in Switzerland is *expert determination*, frequently used in relation to price adjustment disputes, in particular in M&A transactions.

2.10.4 Supervisory Commissions

[364] Harmful cartels are combated by the *SCC* which also has the task of monitoring dominant companies for signs of anticompetitive conduct, of enforcing merger control legislation and of preventing the imposition of restraints of competition by the state (for instance with administrative sanctions). Decisions and rulings of the SCC can be appealed (*see* paragraphs [415] et seq.) to the Swiss Federal Administrative Court (FAC). Decisions of the *FAC* are in turn subject to review by the *SFSC*. However, third parties or competitors cannot challenge a clearance notice or decision of the SCC. Criminal sanctions imposed by the PC may be reviewed by the Federal Criminal Court by means of a complaint.

[365] The *TOB* is a federal commission established under the FMIA. The TOB must, in each case, ensure compliance with the rules applicable to public offers (*see* paragraph [219]). It can impose sanctions, such as the suspension of voting rights or the prohibition of the acquisition of further shares, and it can notify the competent prosecution authorities of general felonies or misdemeanours or of infringements of the FMIA. An appeal against decisions of the TOB may be lodged with *FINMA* within a period of five trading days; such an appeal will usually cause the suspension of proceedings and result in a delay of the takeover process. An appeal against FINMA rulings can be made to the *FAC* within ten calendar days; it generally does not have a suspensive effect. An appeal to the SFSC is not possible.

2.10.5 Enforcement

In General

[366] *Monetary judgments* are enforced as debt collection. Debts – irrespective of their basis, i.e., whether they are based on an enforceable judgment or merely on a disputed claim – are pursued *through the governmental Debt Collection Office* at the debtor's domicile.

[367] Under certain conditions, the debtor is subject to *bankruptcy* proceedings, for instance, if the debtor is a legal entity. In such case, the creditor must file a petition for bankruptcy with the court and the judge has to declare the debtor bankrupt if the debt is not paid by a final deadline. In bankruptcy, all debts become due immediately and are divided into three groups: employees of the debtor, among others, are included in the first group, while social insurance, for instance, is included in the second group, and all other creditors are included in the third group. A receiver (or bankruptcy administrator) is appointed who must sell all the debtor's assets in order to satisfy the creditors, first the creditors in the first group, then the creditors in the second group, and finally, if any funds are left, the creditors in the third group, with whatever funds are left over divided evenly. All other debtors who are not subject to bankruptcy proceedings face an *asset seizure* equivalent to the value of the creditor's debt.

[368] If there is good cause to suspect *over-indebtedness* of a company and the interim balance sheet shows that the claims of the company's creditors are not covered, the board of directors must notify the court unless certain company creditors subordinate their claims to those of all other company creditors to the extent of the capital deficit.

[369] For a *clawback* when certain transactions have been made prior to a bankruptcy *see* paragraphs [188] et seq.

[370] *Non-monetary judgments* are enforceable either directly as specified in the court decision or indirectly, via a court that is competent to order enforcement measures. Often, criminal sanctions are threatened in order to ensure compliance by the obligated party with the judgment (for instance: *The defendant (vendor) is prohibited from continuing to compete with the sold business under threat of punishment pursuant to Article 292 Penal Code and a fine of CHF1 000.00 per day in the event of a violation*).

[371] The *recognition and enforcement of foreign judgments* depend on the countr where they were rendered and whether there is a treaty with Switzerland. Judg ments from Member States of the LugConv will be recognised and enforced i Switzerland without a review of the substance of the judgment, apart from narrow defined exceptions. Recognition of judgments from other countries is regulated b the PILA and is granted when the decision is final and the defendant fails to prov one of the following: that they were not duly summoned; that the foreign decisio was rendered in violation of fundamental principles of Swiss procedural law (fo instance, when the right to be heard was denied); that the matter was either subje to other proceedings brought in Switzerland first or was adjudicated by anoth court; or that recognition is contrary to Swiss public policy. However, reciprocity not required. Once a decision is recognised under the PILA, it is enforced in th same way as a domestic judgment.

[372] Switzerland is a party to the *Convention on the Recognition and Enforcement Foreign Arbitral Awards Concluded in New York in 1958 (New York Convention).* Swi legislation applies the New York Convention regardless whether the country whe the seat of arbitration is located is a party to this convention. The party seeking t enforce the award does not have to obtain a declaration of enforceability from th court at the arbitration venue.

Enforceability of Key Contractual Provisions in Particular

[373] As a general rule where Swiss law is applicable to a transaction, the followin has to be noted unless a particular warranty clause is included in the sales contrac in share deals, the warranty covers only the shares rather than the company; in a asset deal, the warranty in kind comprises solely the specific assets that are sold, bu not the lease of the business premises (which, for instance, might be contaminate with asbestos). Contractual clauses which *specify the scope of the warranty* are nece sary in order to be able to assert claims.

[374] Furthermore, Swiss law does not make the seller liable (a) for defects know to the buyer at the time of purchase or (b) for defects that any normally attentiv buyer should have discovered unless the seller assured the buyer that defects do n exist. If the sales contract does not define the knowledge of the buyer, the selle might allege and try to show with evidence (for instance, presentations, memo randa, emails, testimonies) that a buyer had or should have had *knowledge of a defe* in order to contest a claim. The buyer, on the other hand, will try to qualify eac comment once given by someone of the seller as representation and warrant needless to say, such allegations and lengthy evidence proceedings could b avoided with a *respective restriction of the given representations and warranties* in the co tract.

[375] In a share deal, usually the *company itself does not give representations and wa ranties* to the buyer, since it is of no use: the buyer is not interested in suing its ow company. In addition, an indemnification obligation against the target may be lin ited or forbidden if deemed to constitute a dividend or reimbursement of the shar capital.

[376] For defects liability, Swiss law differentiates between *rescission* of the sale, *reduction* of the price and *compensation* of further damages. The courts are very reluctant to grant a rescission since the company once rescinded after several years of litigation will not be the same company as it was when transferred under the sales contract. And Swiss law encourages the court to order a reduction in the price of the object if it does not consider rescission justified by the circumstances. However, further (or indirect) damage can only be sought in a case of rescission, and such claim can be challenged with proof by the seller that no fault is attributable to it. A claim for direct damage can be made for both the rescission and the price deduction; in the latter case the seller can contest the damage claim with proof that it was acting independently of negligence. It is always very difficult to differentiate between direct and indirect damage. On top, the damage sought must be proven in the wealth of the buyer although, primarily, it has occurred in the wealth of the company. In most contracts, however, the rescission and reduction provided by law are excluded and replaced by a contractual liability, sometimes even with a liability cap and/or with a partial indemnity, all connected to a certain period of time. Often, the seller accepts a contractual obligation to pay a certain amount when a specific risk becomes concrete. Such guarantee is frequently used for tax indemnity, environmental pollution, third-party claims, and violations of the law (e.g., competition law and/or compliance rules).

[377] Typically, fundamental representations should be *valid* for an agreed term of *three – ten years* while the other representation is valid for *twelve to twenty-four months*. In any case, for a notice of breach the given time is to be observed, otherwise a claim for warranty will be dismissed.

[378] Another issue that often arises is whether all sellers are treated equally or whether just some of the sellers should have *joint and several liability*. In a share acquisition, the representations and warranties are normally restricted to the controlling shareholders. A minority shareholder only gives representations and warranties to the target itself (for instance to the incorporation or due organisation, to ownership of the shares, etc.) and not for matters which relate to the day-to-day operations of the company. Consequently, the minority shareholder is excluded from joint liability with the majority shareholder.

Protection of Minority Shareholder Rights

[379] Company law for Ltds (part of the CO) grants various rights to differently defined shareholder minorities:

> Shareholders who represent alone or as a group 10% of the nominal capital stock can request (a) the convocation of a general meeting and/or (b) the inclusion of an item on the agenda of a general meeting; such demand for an agenda item can also be made by shareholders representing together shares with a nominal value of at least CHF 1 million, irrespective of whether the threshold of 10% is met, for instance, applicable to a large company. Where the board of directors fails to grant such a request, the respective shareholders

can call the court at the registered seat to order that a general meeting be co vened.

[380] The implementation of an *ordinary audit* can be requested by shareholde with 10% of the nominal capital stock, even if the ordinary audit is not required law and even if the other 90% of shareholders do not want an ordinary aud Where no auditors have been elected and registered with the Commercial Regist such authority can be informed and asked to intervene. Another possibility open the 10% shareholders is to reject the annual accounts that have not been audit and then to challenge in court the resolution of the general meeting approving t annual accounts.

[381] At the general meeting, shareholders in order to exercise their rights a entitled to *information* from the board of directors about the affairs of the compa and from the auditors about the *methods and results of their audit*. This informati may be refused if it would jeopardise the company's trade secrets or other intere warranting protection. Where information or inspection is refused without ju cause, the shareholder may apply to the court and seek an order for the provisi of appropriate information.

[382] If necessary, shareholders who have already exercised their right to inform tion and inspection and provided that such information is necessary for the exe cise of their rights can demand in a general meeting that a *special auditor* appointed for the clarification of specific matters. If the general meeting approv such a request, either the company or each shareholder can seek the appointme of a special auditor by the court. If the general meeting rejects the request, shar holders who represent 10% of the nominal capital stock or shares with a nomir value of at least CHF2 m can call the court to appoint a special auditor. In a co action, the company might be held to make an advance payment and bear t costs.

[383] If an entity is exempt from the duty to prepare *consolidated accounts*, shar holders who represent at least 20% of the share capital can require the preparati of consolidated accounts. If, thereafter, the entity fails to generate consolidat accounts, each shareholder can challenge the forthcoming general meeting whe the consolidated accounts had to be approved with a court action.

[384] Shareholders together representing at least 10% of the nominal capital sto may request the *dissolution of the company* for good cause by court judgment. Becau this is the last option, the court may order a different solution if appropriate a conscionable for the company and the other shareholders.

[385] In addition, there is a *whole series of general meeting resolutions which requir qualified quorum* of the represented shares (at least two-thirds of the voting righ and an absolute majority of the nominal value of shares) and whose disregard c be challenged in court: any amendment of the company's purpose, the introdu tion of shares with preferential voting rights, any restriction on the transferabil of registered shares, an authorised or contingent capital increase, a capital increa funded by equity capital, against contributions in kind or to fund acquisitions kind and the granting of special privileges, any restriction or cancellation of subscription rights, a relocation of the registered office of the company, or the dissolution of the company. Several decisions require the consent of all shareholders, for instance, the transformation of the company into a non-profit organisation, the consolidation of shares, or the abandonment of a limited audit for a company that does not have more than ten full-time employees on annual average. Finally, companies are free to amend their articles of association with a quorum for various resolutions to improve minority rights, for instance, a seat on the board, among others.

[386] For SMEs, *corporate governance* recommendations for boards of directors are drafted. However, they can only come into force if included in the articles of association, in the internal regulations or in a shareholders' agreement.

Squeeze-Out of Minority Shareholders under Takeover Law

[387] A bidder in a takeover who holds 98% of the voting rights of the target following completion of its bid has the right to seek from the court the cancellation of the remaining equity securities of the target company against the same consideration as offered under the bid (*see also* paragraphs [270] et seq.). It is not totally clear whether the provisions allowing courts to cancel shares remain applicable to non-listed companies after a successful takeover bid. Therefore, bidders often choose to maintain the listing of the target company's shares during squeeze-out court proceedings. The SIX Swiss Exchange agrees to exempt the target company from the duty to publish financial statements in accordance with the listing rules from the completion of the bid until the squeeze-out court decision becomes effective.

2.10.6 Confidentiality

[388] The SCCP requires *civil court proceedings* and the delivery of *judgments* to be *public*. Copies of judgments of the second instance courts and of the SFSC can be requested by anyone and are frequently published online in anonymised form. However, briefs and documents filed by the parties and the court's deliberations are kept confidential.

[389] In contrast to court proceedings, *arbitration* is conducted *privately and confidentially*. However, appeals against a finding of an arbitral tribunal made to a public court are exposed to disclosure just like appeals in civil court proceedings.

3 MERGER CONTROLS, ANTITRUST AND COMPETITION ISSUES

(by Christian Wind)

3.1 Relevant Legislation and Competent Authorities

3.1.1 Legislative Provisions Covering Merger Control and Its Authority

[390] The relevant legislative provisions covering merger control in Switzerland are:

- the *Anti-Cartels Act*; and
- the *Merger Control Ordinance.*

[391] The competent authority is the *SCC* and its secretariat (https://www.weko. admin.ch/weko/en/home.html).

3.1.2 Authorities Involved

[392] In Switzerland, generally, only the SCC is involved.

[393] However, in case of any notifications of planned concentrations involving banks, the SCC will immediately inform FINMA of any such notifications.

[394] For an international merger, one has to check in addition to the Swiss criteria also the relevant criteria and thresholds of other potentially relevant jurisdictions to see if any additional filing abroad might be required.

3.1.3 Mandatory Obligations and Voluntary Filings

[395] Planned concentrations of undertakings must be notified to the SCC before their implementation if, during the financial year preceding the concentration:

(a) the undertakings concerned together reported a turnover of at least *CHF bn*, or a turnover in Switzerland of at least *CHF500 m*; and
(b) at least two of the undertakings concerned each reported a turnover in Switzerland of at least *CHF100 m*.

[396] In the case of *insurance companies*, 'turnover' is replaced by 'annual gross insurance premium income', and in the case of banks and other financial intermediaries who are subject to the accounting regulations set out in the Banking Act, by 'gross income'.

[397] Independent of the thresholds above, notification is also mandatory if one of the undertakings concerned has in proceedings under the Anti-Cartel Act in a final and non-appealable decision been held to be *dominant in a market* in Switzerland

and if the concentration concerns either that market or an adjacent market or a market upstream or downstream thereof.

[398] In case of any uncertainty, the Secretariat of the SCC provides *opinions* and advises undertakings on matters relating to the Anti-Cartel Act.

3.1.4 Mandatory Suspension Obligation Before the Transaction May Be Lawfully Implemented

[399] The undertakings concerned must refrain from implementing the concentration for one month following the notification, unless the SCC has at their request authorised them to do so for good cause or decides to start an investigation.

[400] The legal effect of a concentration that has to be notified is suspended, subject to expiry of the deadline set out in the Anti-Cartel Act and any provisional authorisation to implement the concentration. If the SCC does not take a decision before expiry of the deadline set out in the Anti-Cartel Act, the concentration is deemed authorised, unless the SCC asserts by way of ruling that it has been prevented from conducting the investigation for reasons attributable to the undertakings concerned.

3.2 Scope of the Controls

[401] Concentrations that have to be notified will be investigated by the SCC if a preliminary assessment reveals that they *create or strengthen a dominant position*.

[402] The SCC may prohibit a concentration or authorise it subject to conditions and obligations if the investigation indicates that the concentration:

(a) creates or strengthens a dominant position liable to eliminate effective competition; and
(b) does not improve the conditions of competition in another market such that the harmful effects of the dominant position can be outweighed.

[403] If a concentration of *banks* within the meaning of the Banking Act is deemed necessary by FINMA for reasons related to creditor protection, the interests of creditors may be given priority. In these cases, FINMA takes the place of the SCC, which it will invite to submit an opinion.

[404] In assessing the effects of a concentration on the effectiveness of competition, the SCC also takes account of any market developments and the position of the undertakings in relation to international competition.

[405] A concentration of undertakings that has been prohibited in accordance with Article 10 Anti-Cartel Act may be authorised by the Federal Council at the request of the undertakings involved if, in exceptional cases, it is necessary for compelling reasons of public interest.

[406] The following deals are subject to the relevant merger control laws: The la applies not only to (i) a *merger* but also (ii) a situation where two or more underta ings want to acquire *joint control over a business* which they previously did not joint control or (iii) a situation where *two or more undertakings establish a business that th intend to control jointly*.

[407] *Ad (i):* An undertaking acquires control over a previously independent bus ness as defined by Article 4 paragraph 3 (b) Anti-Cartel Act if it can exercise a dec sive influence over the activities of the other business by the acquisition of righ over shares or by any other means. The means of obtaining control may in partic lar involve the acquisition of the following, either individually or in combinatio ownership rights or rights to use all or parts of the assets of an undertaking and/ rights or agreements which confer a decisive influence on the composition, delil erations, or decisions of the governing bodies of a business.

[408] *Ad (ii):* A situation whereby two or more undertakings acquire joint contr over a business which they previously did not jointly control will be deemed to be concentration of undertakings if the joint venture performs all the functions of a autonomous economic entity on a lasting basis.

[409] *Ad (iii):* If two or more undertakings establish a business which they intend t control jointly, this constitutes a *concentration of undertakings* if the joint venture pe forms the functions set out in the above paragraph and if business activities from a least one of the controlling undertakings are transferred to the joint venture.

3.3 Process and Mechanics

3.3.1 In General

[410] On receiving notification of a planned concentration of undertakings, th SCC decides if there are grounds for conducting an investigation. The SCC notifi the undertakings concerned with the opening of an investigation *within one month receiving the notification*. If no such notice is given within that time period, the co centration may be implemented without reservation.

[411] The undertakings concerned must refrain from implementing the conce tration for one month following the notification unless the SCC has at their reque authorised them to do so for good cause.

[412] If the SCC decides to conduct an investigation, the Secretariat publishes th principal terms of the notification of the concentration and states the time fran within which third parties may comment on the notified concentration.

[413] At the outset of the investigation, the SCC decides whether the concentra tion may by way of exception be implemented provisionally or whether it shou remain suspended.

[414] The SCC will complete its investigation *within four months* unless prevente from doing so for reasons attributable to the undertakings concerned.

[415] If the SCC has prohibited a concentration, the undertakings concerned may, within thirty days, submit to the Federal Department of Economic Affairs, Education and Research an application for exceptional authorisation by the Federal Council for compelling reasons of public interest. If such an application is submitted, the period in which an appeal may be filed with the FAC begins to run only after the parties have been notified of the Federal Council's decision.

[416] Applications for exceptional authorisation by the Federal Council can also be submitted within thirty days of the entry into effect of a judgment of the FAC or the SFSC.

[417] If possible, the Federal Council takes its decision within four months of receipt of the application.

[418] In case of uncertainty, the Secretariat of the SCC provides opinions and advises undertakings on matters relating to the Anti-Cartel Act.

3.3.2 Deals Likely to Be Refused/Rejected

[419] Concentrations that *create or strengthen a dominant position* are likely to be refused.

[420] According to the practice of the SCC, *market shares below 30%* are regularly unproblematic and there is no further investigation.

[421] Market shares *between 30% and 50%* can become an issue, especially when there are specific circumstances which may indicate the existence of a dominant position, such as the existence of capacity constraints or the number of remaining competitors and their respective market shares.

[422] Due to their size, market shares of more *than 50%* are sufficient to indicate a dominant position. If there is a market share of 50% or higher, the situation on the relevant market will usually require further investigation.

[423] The market share is particularly important with regard to the market structure or the ratio of the market shares of the other competitors in the relevant market. In practice, the so-called Herfindahl-Hirschman Index (HH Index), which measures the degree of concentration of a market, is often used to assess this market. While the HH Index was regularly used in the practice of the European Commission, it has to date received little attention from the SCC in Switzerland.

[424] Aspects like *foreign ownership* issues or *protected* sectors do not play a relevant role and are therefore not generally considered.

3.3.3 Views of Trade Competitors or Other Stakeholders

[425] In certain cases, the Secretariat of the SCC may and is authorised to request parties to agreements, undertakings with market power, undertakings concerned in concentrations and affected third parties like competitors, key accounts or key suppliers to provide the competition authorities with all the information required for their investigations and to produce the necessary documents.

[426] Any undertaking that does not, or does not entirely fulfil its obligation provide information or produce documents will be charged up to CHF100 000.

3.3.4 Scope for Offering Remedies to Obtain Clearance

[427] The SCC expects proposals for measures as follows or may even order t following measures by way of a ruling:

(a) the *separation* of any combined undertakings or assets;
(b) the *cessation* of the controlling influence;
(c) other *measures* to restore effective competition.

3.3.5 Sanctions for Breaching Merger Control or Other Antitrust Laws

[428] If a concentration that should have been notified has been implement without due notification, the procedure set out in the Anti-Cartel Act is initiated officio. In this case, the time period set out in the Anti-Cartel Act begins to run soon as the authority possesses all the information that would have to be provid in a notification of a concentration.

[429] The *SCC may revoke* an authorisation *or* decide to investigate a concentrati despite the expiry of the deadline set out in the Anti-Cartel Act if:

(a) the undertakings concerned have provided inaccurate information;
(b) the authorisation was obtained fraudulently; or
(c) the undertakings concerned are in serious breach of a condition attached the authorisation.

[430] The *Federal Council may revoke* an exceptional authorisation on the sar grounds.

[431] If a prohibited concentration has been implemented or if a concentration prohibited after its implementation and exceptional authorisation for the conce tration has not been requested or granted, the undertakings concerned a required to take the necessary steps to restore effective competition.

[432] The SCC may require the undertakings concerned to make binding propc als as to how effective competition may be restored. It will set them a deadli within which to do so.

[433] If the SCC accepts the proposed measures, it may decide how and by wh the undertakings concerned must implement them.

[434] If the undertakings concerned do not make any proposals despite bei required to do so by the SCC, or if the proposals are not accepted by the SCC, t SCC may order the following measures by way of a ruling:

(a) the separation of any combined undertakings or assets;
(b) the cessation of the controlling influence;
(c) other measures to restore effective competition.

[435] Any undertaking that implements a concentration that should have been notified without filing a notification, fails to observe the suspension obligation *(gun jumping)*, fails to comply with a condition attached to the authorisation, implements a prohibited concentration, or fails to implement a measure intended to restore effective competition will be *fined up to CHF1 m.*

[436] In case of repeated failure to comply with a condition attached to the authorisation, the undertaking will be *fined up to 10% of the total turnover in Switzerland* generated by all the undertakings concerned.

3.4 Anticompetitive Restraints

3.4.1 Information Exchange Before Notification

[437] A notification in connection with a planned business combination also includes internal business secrets such as sales figures and the like. Particularly in the case of major mergers, care must be taken to ensure that the companies involved do not provide each other with all relevant business information, as this could be regarded as an *inadmissible exchange* of information as defined by Article 5 Anti-Cartel Act. In practice, it is customary for sensitive information of the participating companies to be disclosed only to the *clean team members* involved and for the companies not to exchange figures with each other.

3.4.2 Non-competing Undertakings for the Vendor and/or Key Employees

[438] Obligations for the vendor and/or for key employees to refrain from competing with the business sold are permissible insofar as they are directly related to the implementation of the proposed concentration and are necessary in terms of the geographical, *time and material dimension* involved.

3.4.3 Limitations on the Permissible Duration

[439] In terms of time, a *non-competition clause* of up to three years is justified if goodwill and know-how are transferred; if only goodwill is transferred, the maximum permissible period is two years.

3.4.4 Individual or Block Exemptions Provided for by Law

[440] Under Swiss law, there are the following notices provided by the SCC (https://www.weko.admin.ch/weko/de/home/dokumentation/bekanntmachungen---erlaeuterungen.html):

(1) Vertical notice
(2) Vehicle notice
(3) SMEs notice
(4) Announcement of homologation and sponsoring of sports articles
(5) Notice on the use of calculation aids.

3.4.5 Relevant Competition Authorities for This Purpose

[441] The competent authority is the same, namely the SCC (https://www.weko admin.ch/weko/en/home.html).

4 TAXATION ASPECTS

4.1 Nature of the Swiss Tax Regime

(by Michael Barrot)

[442] The mild tax climate for companies, entrepreneurs and individuals togethe with the advantage of being able to obtain binding advance tax rulings in genera makes Switzerland a preferred destination for any kind of international business In this regard, Switzerland provides for a highly certain and stable tax environmen and can regularly attract investors to invest and regional headquarters to establis corporate functions in Switzerland.

[443] The codified tax law at the different levels (federal, cantons, and municipali ties) is not very detailed compared to the tax legislations of many other industria lised countries and can therefore be considered as straight-forward and simpl structured. Hence, the tax administrations at different levels enjoy a considerabl degree of discretion in the application of the tax laws. These laws are open enoug to allow the cantonal authorities, within certain limits, to negotiate and enter int *binding advance tax rulings* with individual and corporate taxpayers who are subjec to their tax jurisdiction. This practice, which is very well known, is often used i order to obtain certainty with regard to the tax treatment of a specific transactio Usually, the tax ruling procedure takes just a few weeks and is regularly part of th overall transaction work. The Swiss tax authorities at the federal as well as at th cantonal and municipal levels are bound by a valid tax ruling for as long as the fact and circumstances have been properly documented.

[444] Due to these excellent investment conditions, many multinational group based in Switzerland have successfully grown and reached their current size such a Nestlé, ABB, Swatch Group, Glencore, Novartis, Swiss Re, Roche, Credit Suisse

UBS, etc. Further, many foreign multinationals have domiciled their European or Europe, Middle-East & Africa (EMEA) headquarters in Switzerland for further expansion

4.2 Liability to Tax

[445] Switzerland has a strongly federalist structure, which becomes evident also in its taxation system. While the levy of certain, primarily indirect taxes (Value Added Tax (VAT), stamp taxes, WHT on dividends, etc.) is reserved to the Swiss federal government, other taxes – primarily direct taxes on income – are levied not only by the Swiss federal government but also at the levels of the cantons and the municipalities. The legislative power with regard to cantonal and municipal taxes generally lies with the legislative bodies of the 26 Swiss cantons. Although there is a federal law aiming at harmonising the cantonal tax laws, in actual fact there is still a considerable variety of different cantonal tax systems and rules. In particular, the endeavours to harmonise cantonal and municipal tax rules have to date not included tax rates. As a result, the effective income and capital tax burden varies considerably from canton to canton and even between the municipalities of a given canton.

4.2.1 Tax Residence and Fiscal Domicile

[446] Legal entities, i.e., Ltds, LLCs, cooperatives, associations and foundations, are subject to Swiss federal, cantonal and municipal corporate income tax if they are resident, i.e., if they are incorporated or effectively managed and controlled, in Switzerland.

[447] Legal entities not incorporated and not effectively managed in Switzerland may to a certain extent be subject to Swiss federal, cantonal and municipal corporate income tax if they have a *PE* or *a fixed place of business* (such as a branch) located in Switzerland. Therefore, any profits and gains attributed to such a PE or fixed place of business of a foreign corporate entity are treated the same way as described for Swiss tax-resident legal entities. However, as there are no dividend distributions from a PE or a fixed place of business, Swiss WHT generally does not apply with regard to the repatriation of funds.

[448] In order to avoid qualification as a PE or a fixed place of business, such local presence should follow the applicable double tax treaty and local Swiss tax law, further supported by the recommendations and guidelines of the OECD (e.g., no authority to conclude or negotiate contracts in the name of the foreign legal entity, any competence is strictly limited to marketing and promotion activities).

4.2.2 Taxation of Profits

Calculation of Taxable Profit

[449] Swiss resident companies are generally liable for federal, cantonal an municipal taxes on their *worldwide income*. At the cantonal/municipal level, comp nies also owe an annual capital tax on their net equity (paid-in share capital, su plus and retained earnings). Depending on the canton, the effective capital ta burden may range from 0.01% to 1%.

[450] Income and capital attributable to a foreign PE or foreign real estate exempt from Swiss taxes; it is, however, taken into consideration in determining th applicable cantonal/municipal tax rate in cantons that apply a graduated corpora income tax rate.

[451] The income tax liability of each resident company of a group of compani (whether Swiss or foreign controlled) is calculated based on the net profit shown i its statutory financial statements (*'Massgeblichkeitsprinzip'*, subject to possible adjus ments for tax purposes). If the company does not comply with *Swiss tax accountin principles* in preparing its statutory financial statements, certain differences in th timing of recognition of specific profits and losses may be applied for tax purpos compared to the commercial accounts.

[452] Income from qualifying participations ($x \geq 10\%$) may benefit from tax reli if certain requirements are met.

Capital and Income

[453] Generally speaking, there is no distinction between the taxation of incom and of capital gains at the level of companies. However, certain differences ma occur in connection with the participation exemption regime.

Tax Rates

[454] At the federal level, corporate taxpayers are subject to a flat rate of 8.5% o their taxable income (net profit). Please note that it is possible to deduct the ta charges itself from taxable income under Swiss tax law. Therefore, the effective ta rate is 7.83% of the annual net profit.

[455] In connection with the cantons and the municipalities, who can set their ta rates at their own discretion according to Swiss tax legislation, the aggregate effe tive corporate federal, cantonal and municipal corporate income tax rate may va between approximately 12% and 25%.

Compliance and Administration

[456] The corporate tax return has to be filed on an annual basis upon completio of the relevant business year. Extensions for later filing are available and wide used. During the business year, provisional taxes may be due which are usual invoiced on an estimate basis (down payments) or have to be provisioned for in the accounts.

[457] Swiss tax law does not foresee a specific pre-scheduled cycle for tax audits. However, each company is subject to an audit from time to time.

4.2.3 Other Taxes

[458] Swiss resident companies may, based on their business operations, be subject to further Swiss taxes, of which the most relevant can be summarised as follows.

Capital Tax

[459] The *corporate capital tax* is a cantonal and municipal tax levied on the net capital, consisting of paid-in share capital, surplus and retained earnings or on the dotation capital of Swiss PEs of foreign companies. No such tax is levied at the federal level.

Real Estate Capital Gains Tax

[460] Some cantons know a specific *real estate capital gains tax* that applies upon disposal of Swiss real estate. Real estate capital gains tax is levied on the capital gains on real estate that is situated within the territory of the respective canton. The applicable tax rate significantly depends on the holding period of the real estate. Some cantons do not levy such specific real estate capital gains tax, but rather treat any realised capital gain as part of the ordinary business income, which is subject to corporate income tax.

Real Estate Transfer Tax

[461] Apart from Zurich, most cantons and/or municipalities know *real estate transfer tax* that applies upon a transfer of Swiss real estate. Real estate transfer tax is levied on the consideration for the real estate and is usually equally or solely borne by the buyer.

Capital Issuance Stamp Duty

[462] The contribution of equity to a Swiss company is generally subject to a *capital issuance stamp duty* at a rate of 1% of the fair market value of the assets paid or contributed. Exemptions from the 1% stamp duty may, however, be available in situations of a corporate reorganisation (merger, spin-off, etc.), certain financial restructurings and where a corporate entity, which was originally incorporated abroad, moves its registered seat and domicile to Switzerland. Furthermore, the first CHF1 m of contributed capital is exempt from stamp duty.

Securities Transfer Stamp Duty

[463] The transfer of securities issued by a Swiss or foreign issuer for a conside ation is subject to *securities transfer stamp duty* if at least one of the parties to, or intermediary in, the transaction is a qualified Swiss securities dealer. The transf stamp duty is calculated on the consideration paid; the tax rates are 0.15% for Sw and 0.30% for foreign securities. The transfer stamp duty is usually equally bor by the two parties involved in the transaction.

VAT

[464] Switzerland imposes VAT on the delivery of goods and services rendered Switzerland. The standard tax rate is 7.7%. Reduced rates apply to specific class of consumables such as food, drinks, medicines, etc. and on tourism services su as hotels, etc.

Taxation at Source

[465] Any Swiss resident employer (e.g., a Swiss resident company) is lega obliged to deduct tax at source *(wage withholding)* from the income of forei employees who do not hold a C permit and to remit such amount to the Swiss t administration. As the employer is jointly liable for the correct and adequa deduction and remittance of the employees' income taxes due, any failure and su sequent non-payment by the respective employees would result in the assumpti of these individuals' tax costs without any guarantee that these costs can recharged to the respective employees.

Social Security Contributions

[466] Any Swiss resident employer (e.g., a Swiss resident company) is lega obliged to deduct from all salary payments, regardless of the migration status of t employee, the *social security contributions* and to remit such amount to the Sw social security administration. The social security contribution which is d amounts to approx. 13% and is in general equally borne by the employer a employee. The employee's portion is directly deducted from the salary payme and the employer's portion is an additional expense for the employer.

[467] As the employer is jointly liable for the correct and adequate deduction a remittance of the employee's contribution, any failure or non-deduction wou result in the assumption of the employee's portion without any guarantee that t cost can be recharged to the respective employees.

Participation Exemption Relief

On Dividends

[468] Tax relief applies to dividend income derived by Swiss resident companies from substantial participations. A participation is considered 'substantial' if it represents control of at least 10% of the share capital or of 10% of the profit entitlements of another company or if it has a fair market value of at least CHF1 m. Such qualifying dividend income may benefit from the *'participation deduction'* (*'Beteiligungsabzug'*), which is equal to the ratio between the 'net participation income' and the total net income of the company. The 'net participation income' is defined as follows:

- Gross dividend income from substantial participations
- non-refundable foreign withholding taxes
- financing costs related to the respective participations
- 5% of the dividend income for covering administrative costs
- 'net participation income'

[469] The deduction ratio so determined is applied to the amount of income tax computed on the total net profit including the qualifying dividend income. The participation deduction is not granted to the extent that the book value of the underlying participation is depreciated due to the dividend distribution.

On Capital Gains

[470] The participation exemption relief can also be claimed in respect of realised capital gains. Tax relief on capital gains is subject to the following prerequisites:

(a) The participation sold must represent at least 10% of the other company's capital or 10% of the company's profit entitlements.
(b) The participation must have been held for at least one year.
(c) The capital gain qualifies for the *'Beteiligungsabzug'* only to the extent that the sales proceeds exceed the investment costs of the participation. Any portion of the gain representing recaptured depreciation does not qualify.

4.3 Tax Consolidation, Group Relief of Gains and Losses

4.3.1 Tax Consolidation

[471] Swiss tax law does not foresee a tax grouping or a loss consolidation for company tax purposes. Each company has to draw up on a stand-alone basis its own financial statements and file its own tax return. Only losses incurred at the level of

PEs (including abroad) may be deducted from the taxable profit. Losses from a foreign PE may be recaptured in order to avoid double deduction of losses abroad and in Switzerland itself. In return, a Swiss PE cannot set off foreign headquarter losses against profits attributable to this PE.

4.3.2 Tax Losses

[472] Swiss companies may offset generated profit against a loss incurred during the *preceding seven years* (tax loss carry-forward). In the event of a recapitalisation, gains from the waiver of debt may be offset for extended periods.

[473] Losses may survive a change of ownership if the ownership was not solely motivated by those existing losses, but rather by commercial interests. Moreover, the target company may even be merged with another group company based on a group-internal reorganisation without jeopardising its existing tax loss carry-forwards.

4.3.3 CFC Legislation

[474] Pursuant to Swiss tax law, there are no specific Controlled Foreign Corporation (CFC) rules with respect to controlled foreign companies. Further, there are also no intentions at all to introduce any CFC legislation in future.

4.4 Tax Considerations Arising on M&A Transactions (Share Deal Versus Asset Deal)

(by Nicola Corvi)

4.4.1 Seller's Considerations

[475] Generally speaking, capital gains realised by an individual on the *disposition of shares* are tax exempt, absent certain limited exceptions, such as the sale of a Swiss real estate company, re-characterisation of the capital gain as an indirect partial liquidation or transposition, if the shares are held as a business asset, or if the seller qualifies as a professional securities dealer.

[476] Capital gains realised by a corporate entity upon the sale of shares in another company are in principle taxable income, but qualify for the participation exemption if the selling corporate entity disposes of at least 10% of the shares in the target, has held these shares for at least one year prior to the sale and the sale proceeds exceed the investment costs of the participation. Recaptured depreciation does not qualify for the participation exemption. On a cantonal level, the sale of the majority of a Swiss real estate company may lead to real estate capital gains tax and transfer tax (so-called economic change of ownership).

[477] Conversely, a *sale of assets and liabilities* by a corporate entity leads to the realisation of built-in gains (so-called hidden reserves) which is subject to corporate income tax. Upon liquidation of the company which has sold its assets and liabilities, the liquidation dividend is considered to be taxable income for the receiving individual shareholders. If said individual shareholders own at least 10% of the dividend-paying company, they may claim a relief of 30% of the dividend subject to tax at the federal level and a deduction for cantonal/municipal tax purposes which varies depending on the canton. If the assets contain real estate, the sale may then again lead to real estate capital gains tax and transfer tax on a cantonal level.

[478] If the shareholder of the company having sold its business is a corporate entity, it may claim a participation exemption with respect to the liquidation dividend, provided it has held at least 10% of the shares in the dividend-paying company.

[479] In a *share for share exchange*, the individual seller realises a tax-free capital gain, provided the shares in the acquiring company received in exchange for the shares of the target company have a nominal value which is equal to or less than the nominal value of the target's shares. If the shares received have a higher value than the ones exchanged, said difference is considered taxable income.

[480] A corporate seller in a share for share transaction will realise a capital gain or loss. With respect to the capital gain, the participation exemption may be claimed if the seller held at least 10% of the shares in the target company. A loss will be deductible from ordinary income.

4.4.2 Buyer's Considerations

[481] Upon the *acquisition of shares*, the buyer will have initial costs of investment equal to the purchase price paid. Even if there is a goodwill portion in the purchase price, it may neither be accounted for separately nor be subject to depreciation. As the tax book value of the assets in the acquired company remains unchanged, the buyer should account for deferred tax liability (resulting from hidden reserves) in the purchase price of the shares.

[482] In case of an *acquisition of assets and liabilities*, the buyer will have a step-up to the fair market value of the business acquired which will form a higher basis for depreciation. Goodwill may be accounted for separately and may be depreciated. Interest on debt incurred for the acquisition of the business may generally be deducted.

[483] Hence, absent special circumstances, the buyer will generally prefer an asset deal whereas the seller, especially if the seller is an individual, will favour a share deal.

4.4.3 Specific Aspects

Tax Losses

[484] In a *share deal*, the target company preserves its tax attributes, including loss carry-forward (losses can be carried forward for a maximum of seven years The change of shareholder neither affects the availability of the tax loss to offs future income nor the residual loss carry-forward period.

[485] In the case of an *asset deal*, the tax loss is no longer available. It may, howeve be used by the seller to offset the realisation of built-in gain on the assets that ar sold.

Debt Financing/Acquisition Costs

[486] In a *share deal*, the debt is incurred by the buyer and does not affect the targ in any way. Hence, the acquiring company needs to comply with thin capitalisatio rules and the deductibility of interest.

[487] In an *asset deal*, the buyer may deduct the interest on the debt incurred fc the acquisition from its taxable income, including the income generated by th newly acquired business, provided that it complies with the thin capitalisatio rules.

[488] In a share deal, the acquisition costs may be deducted by the acquiring con pany, but may not be passed on to the target.

Deferred Payments and Earn Outs

[489] These are not common in Switzerland. Earn outs are agreed upon mainly i transactions concerning SMEs.

[490] In an *asset deal*, a deferred payment will give rise to taxable income for th seller, but will not be tax deductible by the buyer as part of the purchase price.

[491] In the case of a share deal, a deferred payment will be treated as part of th purchase price and thus the buyer will have to increase its initial costs of investme in the shares acquired accordingly, but will not be granted a deduction. The sell will treat the deferred payment in the same manner as the purchase price paid the outset. If the seller is an individual and continues to work for the target, the ta authorities may qualify a part of the purchase price as taxable income.

4.5 Structuring the Investment

[492] Given that there is no tax consolidation available, other ways must be foun to make tax-efficient use of debt interest.

[493] The most obvious solution is a *merger* of the newly acquired subsidiary into i parent (upstream merger). This would allow for the debt interest to be offset, least in part, against the income generated by the merged business. However, in many instances, the tax authorities have questioned the deductibility of acquisition debt interest in such instances.

[494] A subsequent merger of the target into the acquiring company will typically give rise to a merger gain or loss, the amount of which is equal to the difference in the initial cost of investment that the acquiring company had in the shares of the target and the net amount of the target's assets and liabilities. A merger gain is treated as taxable income which qualifies for the participation exemption (cf. paragraph [480]). Conversely, a merger loss is tax deductible only to the extent that there is no built-in gain in the assets and liabilities transferred as a result of the merger (so-called real merger loss).

[495] Furthermore, in case of a sale of shares of a company by an individual seller to a corporate buyer, followed by a merger of the newly acquired company into the buyer within five years after the sale, the issue of a so-called indirect partial liquidation will arise. If the individual seller knew or should have known that the target company's assets will be used to finance the acquisition, in whole or in part, the otherwise tax-free capital gain on the sale of shares may be requalified into taxable income under the indirect partial liquidation statute. Inevitably though, a well-advised individual seller will insist that the share purchase agreement provides a clause prohibiting such a merger.

[496] In any event, the *thin capitalisation rules* (*see* paragraphs [515] et seq.) will have to be complied with.

[497] A merger may be achieved on a tax-free basis if (i) all the assets and liabilities are transferred at book value, i.e., they take a substituted basis in the books of the surviving company, and (ii) the built-in gain on these assets and liabilities remains subject to taxation in Switzerland when and to the extent realised. Given that in a merger all the tax attributes of the merged company are transferred to the surviving company, this applies also to loss carry-forwards, which may thus potentially be used.

[498] In a merger, *VAT* is levied on the transfer of assets. The companies may file a declaration with the tax administration rather than paying the tax.

4.6 Withholding Taxes (WHT)

(by Michael Barrot, Nicola Corvi, Cédric Jenoure, Sascha Wohlgemuth)

4.6.1 General

[499] Swiss WHT is levied on *certain income from movable capital assets*, *winnings* from money games as well as lotteries and games of skill for sales promotion and certain *insurance benefits*. The income deriving from Swiss movable capital which is subject to Swiss WHT includes participation income (including formal or hidden di dends), income from qualifying bonds, certain distributions by collective inve ment schemes as well as interest payments on deposits with Swiss banks.

[500] Therefore, IP *royalties* paid to foreign and domestic recipients as well as royalties received from foreign payers and management or consultancy fees paid foreign recipients as well as payments in respect of the *purchase or renting of immo able property* are generally *not subject to Swiss WHT*. *Interest* payments deriving fro loans (including private, commercial and inter-company loans) that do *not* quali as *bonds* for Swiss WHT purposes are also not subject to Swiss WHT. For Swiss WH purposes, the definition of qualifying bonds is extensive and includes, *inter al* loan debentures and cash debentures. In particular, the distinction between qua fying and non-qualifying bonds requires due consideration on a case-by-case ba and special attention has to be given to mortgage-secured loans. However, roya fees, management or consultancy fees as well as interest income that are not *at arn length* may be treated as hidden dividends for Swiss WHT purposes.

[501] Swiss WHT aims to ensure full taxation of the income of domestic taxpaye and to prevent tax evasion. Provided that the income is properly declared accounted for, Swiss WHT is generally reimbursed in the form of a refund or t credit.

[502] *With regard to non-Swiss resident taxpayers*, Swiss WHT aims to prevent evasi as well as serves fiscal purposes. Generally, a partial or full refund of Swiss WHT available based on a double taxation treaty. However, Swiss WHT constitutes a fin tax burden if a double tax treaty is not available and no tax credit is granted in t country of residence of the recipient.

[503] Dividend distributions in form of the *repayment of nominal share capital* as w as of qualifying capital contribution reserves are *not subject to Swiss WHT*. The cr ation and distribution of qualifying capital contribution reserves require comp ance with some formal requirements. Principally, the repayment of qualifyi capital contributions also does not have any income tax consequences at the le of a Swiss individual taxpayer.

[504] In addition to the partial or full refund of Swiss WHT in the form of a rei bursement, in particular qualifying companies may fulfil the Swiss WHT obligati by applying the notification procedure (i.e., notification of the Swiss Federal T Administration (FTA) replaces the payment of Swiss WHT), which is beneficial f liquidity purposes. By applying the notification procedure, no retention of Sw WHT by the debtor of the taxable income and no refund request by the recipient the taxable income are required. The application of the notification procedure companies requires in particular that the recipient of the income is entitled to t (full) refund of Swiss WHT and holds a direct qualifying participation in the sha capital of the distributing company as well as compliance with specific form requirements. Further, Swiss WHT provides for the application of the notificati procedure in additional cases to be assessed on a case-by-case basis.

[505] *The statutory rate of Swiss WHT* applicable on income from movable assets – in particular dividends and interest payments from qualifying bonds – as well as winnings from money games, lotteries and games of skill for sales promotion is *35%*. Insurance payments are subject to Swiss WHT rates of 8% to 15%. Generally, Swiss WHT has to be withheld at source and be remitted by the debtor of the taxable payment to the FTA. Therefore, the recipient of the taxable payment generally receives 65% of the gross income, net after tax.

[506] The 35% Swiss WHT rate constitutes an obstacle for foreign investors to investing directly in Swiss corporate bonds and equity. However, Switzerland's extensive double tax treaty network provides foreign investors with full or partial relief from the 35% Swiss WHT rate in a cost-efficient and simple procedure. In addition, the application of the notification procedure provides an additional opportunity for avoiding the refund procedure and allows the investor to maintain a beneficial level of liquidity.

[507] Switzerland aims to implement a *reform* of Swiss WHT. The Swiss Parliament approved a reform of Swiss withholding tax. This reform is intended to strengthen the Swiss debt capital markets. One of the measures is the abolition of Swiss withholding tax on all interest income, with the exception of interest income on Swiss bank accounts held by Swiss resident individuals. The reform is subject to popular vote in the second half of 2022. If not rejected in the popular vote, the abolition of Swiss withholding tax on interest payments will take effect on 1 January 2023.

4.6.2 Double Tax Treaties

[508] As said, Switzerland has an extensive network of double tax treaties affecting the payment of Swiss WHT which includes *over 100 countries*, and it actively seeks to extend this network. In general, the double tax treaties concluded by Switzerland follow the OECD model tax treaty.

[509] The double tax treaties apply to persons who are tax residents of the contracting states. In addition, in particular requirements with regard to beneficial ownership and substance as well as compliance with the anti-avoidance rules have to be met. Generally, the exemption of dividends from Swiss WHT requires the direct shareholder to have a qualifying shareholding quota. In that regard, jurisdictions qualifying for an acquisition structure can principally provide for a double tax treaty with a 0% tax rate on dividends. Further, the double tax treaties concluded by Switzerland usually reduce the Swiss WHT rate to be applied to interest income to 0% or 10%.

[510] In general, investment structures use companies such as the Ltd or LLC, and a tax ruling confirming the tax treatment of the investment structure on a case-by-case basis should be obtained in advance. Swiss partnerships are rarely used for investment structures by foreign investors.

4.7 Debt Financing

(by Nicola Corvi)

[511] Debt raised by a Swiss corporate taxpayer from a third party is not subject t any limitations from a Swiss tax perspective. Interest paid on third-party deb qualifies as a tax-deductible expense. However, loans granted to foreigners an secured by immovable property are subject to WHT, unless an applicable doubl tax treaty provides differently.

[512] Inter-company debt obtained by a Swiss corporate taxpayer must be in lin with the Swiss thin capitalisation rules (cf. paragraphs [515] et seq.).

[513] The FTA issues two circular letters per year with safe-haven interest rate applicable to inter-company debt, one for inter-company loans denominated i CHF, another for inter-company loans denominated in foreign currencies. The cir cular letters provide for (i) minimum interest rates on loans from a Swiss corporat taxpayer to a shareholder or related party and (ii) maximum interest rates on loan from a shareholder or related party to a Swiss corporate taxpayer. The safe-have interest rates set forth in the circular letters of the FTA are deemed to be at arm' length. Interest rates that deviate from the safe-haven interest rates annually pub lished by the FTA qualify as tax-deductible expenses, provided that the Swiss cor porate taxpayer provides evidence that the interest rate applied is at arm's length If the interest rates deviate from the safe-haven rules and are not at arm's length the excessive interest rates qualify as hidden profit distributions, are added to th Swiss company's taxable income and are subject to Swiss WHT.

[514] The acquisition of a Swiss target company by means of an acquisition vehicl with a subsequent merger and debt push-down is a commonly used acquisitio structure. The Swiss tax authorities, however, often view acquisition structure involving an acquisition vehicle as a *tax avoidance scheme*. On the basis of the doc trine of tax avoidance, the Swiss tax authorities often disallow the target compan the tax-efficient deduction of interest expenses on the debt pushed down. Gener ally, the Swiss tax authorities assume a tax avoidance scheme if (i) the structure cho sen is uncommon, inappropriate or lacks any economic rationale, (ii) tax saving are the predominant reason for the structure chosen, or (iii) substantial tax saving result from the use of the structure chosen.

4.8 Thin Capitalisation

[515] The Swiss thin capitalisation rules – in the form of safe-haven rules – are se forth in the FTA's circular letter no. 6 of 6 June 1997. The Swiss tax authoritie apply the safe-haven rules of circular letter no. 6 in order to determine whether Swiss corporate taxpayer has been thinly capitalised with equity. According to cir cular letter no. 6, an asset-based ratio approach is applied in order to determin the debt amount accepted under Swiss tax law. The calculation is based on th *respective fair market values* of the assets on the balance sheet of the Swiss corporat taxpayer. The total debt of the Swiss corporate taxpayer should not exceed the aggregate value of each asset item below multiplied by the percentage rate as at the end of a given business year:

- 100% of cash;
- 85% of receivables;
- 85% of inventory;
- 85% of other current assets;
- 90% of bonds issued in Swiss francs;
- 80% of bonds issued in foreign currencies;
- 60% of listed shares;
- 50% of other shares in companies;
- 70% of an investment in participations;
- 85% of loans;
- 50% of machinery and equipment;
- 70% of operating real estate, homes and building land;
- 80% of other immovable property; and
- 70% of other intangibles.

[516] For finance companies, the maximum allowable debt equals 6/7ths of their total assets.

[517] The total sum of the fair market value of the assets multiplied by the above 'safe-haven' percentage rates equals the *maximum allowable debt* under Swiss tax law. If the debt exceeds the maximum allowable debt under Swiss tax law calculated in this way, the difference between the actual debt and the maximum allowable debt under Swiss tax law is qualified as *hidden equity* rather than debt, provided and to the extent that the excessive debt has been granted by a related party/group company. The Swiss corporate taxpayer may, however, provide evidence that the specific inter-company financing or financing from a related party is at arm's length. Loans granted by a third party that are secured by a shareholder or a related party of the Swiss corporate taxpayer are treated as loans from related parties and therefore fall within the scope of the Swiss thin capitalisation rules.

[518] The consequence of the qualification of inter-company debt or debt from a related party as hidden equity is that the Swiss tax authorities *disallow the deduction of the interest* paid by the Swiss corporate taxpayer on the excess debt for the purpose of determining the taxable profit, even if the safe-haven interest rates annually published by the FTA have been applied. Additionally, the *hidden equity is subject to cantonal capital tax*. Finally, the FTA treats the interest payments on the excess debt as hidden profit distributions and levies 35% Swiss – *WHT –*, with the ultimate Swiss WHT burden amounting to *53.8% (as the hidden profit distribution is regarded as being net of the 35% WHT, i.e. 65% of the actual distribution subjected to the WHT)*. Whether the Swiss WHT can be fully or partially reclaimed depends on the applicable double taxation treaty, if any.

4.9 Transfer Pricing

[519] Switzerland has no specific transfer pricing legislation. Furthermore, Swi zerland does not have any specific transfer pricing documentation requirement with the exception of the country-by-country reporting obligations (CbCR). Hov ever, as a member of the OECD, Switzerland adheres to the OECD guidelines o transfer pricing.

[520] In 1997, the FTA informed the cantonal tax authorities that they had to tak into consideration the OECD transfer pricing guidelines for multinational ente prises and tax administrations when taxing multinational enterprises. In 2004, th FTA issued a circular letter to the cantonal tax authorities – replacing the 1997 ci cular letter – reminding them that the OECD transfer pricing guidelines must b considered. In its case law, the SFSC refers to the principle of dealing at arm length as a fundamental principle of Swiss tax law.[1]

[521] When a transfer price does not observe the principle of dealing at arm length, then the Swiss tax authorities will adjust the taxable profit on the basis c Article 58 of the Federal Act on Direct Tax and Article 24 of the Federal Act on th Harmonisation of Direct Taxes. The aforementioned norms only allow comme cially justifiable costs as tax-deductible expenses. The *burden of proof* for demo strating that a transfer price is an *arm's length* price lies with the *Swiss corpora taxpayer*.

[522] If an inappropriate transfer price results in a reduction of the taxable prof of the Swiss corporate taxpayer for the benefit of its shareholder or a related part the FTA treats the difference between the transfer price applied and the arm length price as a *hidden profit distribution* and levies 35% Swiss WHT, with the ult mate Swiss WHT burden amounting to 53.8%. Whether the Swiss WHT can be ful or partially reclaimed depends on the applicable double taxation treaty, if any.

[523] Swiss tax law does not provide for specific transfer pricing audits. Transfe prices are generally *audited in the course of regular tax audits*. Cantonal tax authoriti have increasingly become more aggressive when auditing transfer prices involvin inter-company transactions regarding IP or foreign group companies with a ba ance sheet loss.

[524] Advance pricing agreements (unilateral, bilateral and multilateral) may b negotiated with the Swiss tax authorities. Furthermore, it is common practice i Switzerland to obtain a tax ruling with respect to inter-company transactions.

[525] Switzerland has actively been involved in the Base Erosion and Profit Shif ing (BEPS) project of the OECD, in which the OECD aims at achieving tax tran parency and a level playing field with respect to multinational enterprise Switzerland has committed itself to implementing the minimum standards of th BEPS action plan in domestic legislation. Some BEPS project outcomes hav already been incorporated in the Federal Act on Tax Reform and Swiss Act on O Age and Survivors' Insurance (AHVG) Financing that has entered into force on January 2020 such as the abolishment of privileged tax regimes (holding, domici and mixed companies) that were no longer internationally recognised and th introduction of new, internationally recognised rules such as the patent box regime and a special deduction for research and development expenses at the cantonal level.

5 EMPLOYMENT CONSIDERATIONS

(by Tobias Herren)

5.1 Legislative Framework

[526] The main legislative framework is provided by Articles 319–362 CO, the *Swiss Employment Act* and its ordinance, and the *Swiss Secondment Act*.

5.2 Employment Protection

5.2.1 In Case of a Business Transfer

[527] Where the employer transfers the company or a part thereof to a third party, the employment relationship and all attendant rights and obligations *pass to the buyer* as of the date of the transfer, unless the employee refuses such transfer. In the event that the employee refuses the transfer, the employment relationship ends on expiry of the statutory notice period; until then, the buyer and the employee are obliged to perform the contract. Hence, if the buyer needs specific employees, it is advisable to obtain their consent prior to the transfer.

[528] Where the transferred relationship is governed by a *collective employment contract*, the buyer is obliged to abide by it for one year unless it expires or is terminated sooner.

[529] The former employer and the buyer are jointly and severally *liable for any claims* of an employee which fell due prior to the transfer or which fall due between that time and the date on which the employment relationship could normally be terminated or is terminated following refusal of the transfer.

[530] In Switzerland, it is rather uncommon that employees are entitled to *management representation* (i.e., to have a seat on the company board). However, in bigger companies this might be the case due to internal regulations.

[531] In case of a *transfer of shares or the sale of a business*, the *employer must inform* the organisation that represents the employees or, where there is none, the employees themselves in good time *before the transfer takes place* about the reason for the transfer and its legal, economic and social consequences for the employees. In good time means prior to the transfer itself, but not prior to the decision which led to the transfer. If the transfer involves measures affecting the employees, the organisation that represents the employees or, where there is none, the *employees* themselves *must* *be consulted* in good time *before the relevant decisions are taken*. In good time th means that the workforce must be granted enough time to study the received infc mation, to formulate concrete proposals and to present these to the employer. Fu thermore, the employer has to have enough time to examine these proposals ar respond to them before it draws its final conclusions and takes the relevant de sions.

[532] If the employees or their representation have not been duly consulted, t organisation that represents the employees can request the competent court issue an order prohibiting the registration of a merger or an acquisition in t Commercial Register.

5.2.2 Mass Redundancies

[533] The CO also provides for a *consultation procedure* in case of mass redunda cies. The provisions regarding mass redundancies are applicable if notices of tern nation are given within thirty days of each other for reasons not pertaini personally to the employees (e.g., economic reasons) and which affect (1) at lea ten employees in a business normally employing more than 20 and fewer than 1(employees; (2) at least 10% of the employees of a business normally employing least 100 and fewer than 300 employees; (3) at least 30 employees in a busine normally employing at least 300 employees. Although the obligation to consu with the employees does not restrict the employer's right to dismiss employees p se, the employer or the buyer may have to pay compensation for unlawful termin tion not exceeding two months' salary.

[534] Although these consultation procedures are regarded as very important Switzerland, there are no statutory rights given to *work councils* – if at all in place with the exception of a right of information and consultation before a decision taken. Work councils in Switzerland are not vested with rights like in Germar France or the Netherlands.

5.2.3 Protections Mandatory and Modifiable

[535] The CO defines the mandatory protections in Articles 361 et seq. and dra a distinction between provisions from which no derogation is permissible to t detriment of *the employer or the employee* and provisions from which no derogation permissible to the detriment of *the employee*.

[536] According to these provisions, the former employer and the buyer cann derogate their *liability* in the event of a transfer of employment relationships n can they modify their duty to negotiate in order to conclude a social plan in t event of mass redundancies to the detriment of the employee. Furthermore, t compensation in the event of unlawful termination cannot be derogated, neither the detriment of the employer nor the employee.

5.2.4 Termination of Individual Employment Contract

[537] In comparison with other jurisdictions, Swiss law grants a relatively free right of termination with regard to *ordinary termination* (i.e., no particular reason is required). The party giving notice of termination must only state their reasons in writing if the other party so requests.

[538] The employment relationship may be terminated to the end of any calendar month by giving one month's *notice* during the first year of service, two months' notice in the second to ninth years of service, and three months' notice thereafter. These notice periods may be changed by written individual, standard or collective employment contract; however, they can only be reduced to less than one month by collective employment contract and only for the first year of service. To determine the year of service, all of the employee's years are calculated, as all rights and obligations pass to the buyer.

[539] In the case of termination with *immediate effect*, good cause is required or the salary must be at risk. It lies at the discretion of the court to determine whether there is good cause; the threshold is generally quite high.

5.2.5 Rights of Employees Against Dismissal and/or to Compensation on Termination

[540] Any party who terminates the employment relationship unlawfully (e.g., on account of an attribute pertaining to the person of the other party, because the other party exercises a constitutional right, solely in order to prevent claims under the employment relationship from accruing to the other party) must pay *compensation* to the other party if they submit their objection to the notice of termination in writing not later than the end of the notice period and claims for compensation within 180 days of the end of the employment relationship.

[541] In the context of mass redundancies, where termination is unlawful (i.e., violation of the consultation procedure), the compensation may not exceed two months' salary for the employee.

[542] Furthermore, any termination during an *inopportune period* (e.g., during sickness, pregnancy, military service; *see* Article 336c CO for details) is void. By contrast, where such notice was given prior to the commencement of a prescribed period but the notice period has not yet expired at that juncture, it is suspended and does not resume until the prescribed period has ended.

[543] *No derogation* of compensation in the event of unlawful termination is possible to the detriment of the employee or the employer.

[544] The CO does not distinguish per se between 'blue collar workers' and 'white collar workers'. There are, however, several collective employment contracts (e.g., for the construction industry) which comprise regulations especially for 'blue collar workers'.

5.2.6 Relevant Procedures to Be Followed on Termination

[545] Unless agreed otherwise, the termination is not bound to any *legal form* (i.e., can even be made orally). For evidentiary purposes, however, the employer is still advised to terminate the contract in writing and to make sure to have proof that the employee has taken notice (i.e., acknowledgement of receipt, registered letter or delivery in front of witnesses). The party giving notice of termination must only state their reasons in writing if the other party so requests. The party terminating the contract must abide by the aforementioned notice periods.

[546] In many sectors collective employment contracts define *minimum wages*. However, individual employment contracts are still the standard case where salaries are individually agreed. Non-wage labour costs for the employer vary in Switzerland between approx. 8% and 17%, depending on the business sector and age of the employee.

5.2.7 Collective Bargaining Agreements with Local Workforce

[547] It is not normal in Switzerland that employers negotiate collective bargaining agreements with the local workforce. Employers and employees still have a strong preference for individual employment contracts in sectors that are not regulated by collective employment contracts.

[548] *Unions* have certain powers regarding the negotiation of collective employment contracts, but compared to other European countries they are not generally powerful or problematic. The commandment of labour peace means that strikes are extremely rare and are restricted to certain sectors, e.g., construction.

5.3 Pensions

[549] Both the employee and the employer are obliged according to the AHVG to make regular payments to the state pension scheme. In addition, employees above the age of 25 and with an annual income above CHF21 330 are obliged to make additional payments to an occupational benefits plan under the Swiss Act on Occupational Retirement, Survivors' and Disability Pension Plans. The employer who employs an employee who is compulsorily insured must set up or join a pension fund entered in the register for occupational benefits. It is common in Switzerland to divide this contribution payment equally between the employer and the employee.

[550] As of 1 January 2020, both the employee and the employer have to pay 4.35% (8.7% in total) of gross salaries for the AHV. The employer is obliged to withhold 4.35% of gross salaries and then transfer it together with its own part to the respective compensation fund. This obligation applies to all employees working in Switzerland. There are, however, some exceptions pursuant to the bilateral agreements between Switzerland and the EU.

[551] Where the employee is obliged to make contributions to an *occupational benefits scheme* (from an annual salary of CHF21 330; pensionable salary CHF24 885 to CHF85 320), the employer must simultaneously contribute an amount at least equal to the total contributions of all its employees; it must finance its contributions from its own funds or from contribution reserves held by the fund which have previously been accrued by the employer for this purpose and which are reported separately in the fund's accounts. The employer must transfer the contribution deducted from the employee's salary together with its own contribution to the occupational benefits scheme not later than at the end of the first month following the calendar year or insurance year for which the contributions are due.

5.4 Retention of Key Management and Employees

[552] In order to ensure the continuation of individual vendors, members of the management team or other key employees, the buyer of a company has no means other than what is provided by the individual employment contract. In particular, the imposition of non-competition clauses will most likely not be accepted if it is not counterbalanced by a substantial salary increase. However, *non-competition agreements* that are in accordance with the legal provisions and rich trove of case law *are enforceable* by the courts.

5.5 Treatment of Foreign Employees

5.5.1 Overview

[553] With regard to foreign employees, the special political situation of Switzerland must first be taken into account. Switzerland is not a member of the EU. Through numerous *bilateral agreements*, however, it participates in the *EU's internal market*. The free movement of persons to the EU is also regulated in the Agreement on the Free Movement of Persons Concluded Between Switzerland and the European Union (AFMP), which is decisive for employees from an EU Member State; the Swiss Aliens and Integration Act (AIG) only applies in a subsidiary manner or if it contains more favourable provisions for EU citizens. In principle, the AFMP gives EU nationals the right to freely choose their place of work within the territories of the contracting states.

[554] *Third-country nationals*, i.e., employees from non-EU countries, are subject to the stricter Aliens and Integration Act and cannot invoke the AFMP. Only managers, specialists and qualified workers from these countries can be admitted to work in Switzerland.

5.5.2 Conditions for Admission and Permits

EU Citizens

[555] Citizens of the so-called EU-27 (EU countries without Croatia for th moment) and EFTA (Norway, Iceland and Liechtenstein) only need a *residence pe mit*, which is also their work permit. Such a permit is issued when a written decla ration of employment from the employer is available. The following restrictior apply to Croatian nationals: (i) control of the national priority (preferential trea ment of Swiss nationals); (ii) control of wage and working conditions; (iii) separat annually increasing maximum numbers for short-stay and residence permits.

[556] However, a residence permit is only necessary if the stay lasts more tha three months. In the case of a shorter stay, only a *registration procedure* is require (this does not apply to Croatian nationals, who must have a permit regardless of th duration of their stay). For employment of more than three months, employee must register with their municipality of residence and apply for a residence permi Depending on the duration of the employment, a short-term residence permit (sc called L permit, for employment contracts up to one year) or a residence perm (so-called B permit, for permanent employment contracts or those lasting longe than one year) is granted. A permanent residence permit (so-called C permit) ca be applied for after ten years if the restrictive conditions are fulfilled. There ar bilateral agreements with some EU Member States according to which a perma nent residence permit can be issued after five years of residence.

[557] It is also possible to issue a *cross-border commuter permit* (G permit). This pe mit is issued to self-employed and employed EU/EFTA nationals who are resider in the EU/EFTA and return to their place of residence at least once a week.

[558] Service providers from the EU/EFTA area can offer their services in Switze land for ninety calendar days a year *without* the need for *a permit*. However, the must report their service at least eight days before the start of their activity. Th regulation applies to all employees whose companies are based in the EU, irrespe tive of their nationality. In the case of services lasting more than ninety days, th granting of a permit is at the discretion of the authorities.

Non-EU Citizens

[559] As mentioned above, third-country citizens are subject to stricter admissio rules than EU/EFTA citizens. They are only admitted to the labour market if the are well *qualified*, i.e., have a university degree and several years of profession experience.

[560] If an employer wishes to employ a third-country citizen in Switzerland, must prove that a person *suitable* for the vacancy is not available on the domest labour market or on the labour markets of the EU/EFTA countries. In additio wages, social insurance contributions and working conditions must correspond t local, professional and sector-specific conditions in Switzerland.

[561] In contrast to an EU/EFTA citizen, citizens from a non-EU country are not entitled to a work and residence permit. The *granting of the permit* is at the discretion of the authority and is based on the following criteria: (i) the admission of the third-country national is in the interests of Switzerland as a whole and the economy as a whole; (ii) the annual maximum number of admissions laid down by the Swiss government has not yet been reached; (iii) no other persons are available on the domestic labour market and the labour markets of the EU/EFTA countries; (iv) compliance with the reporting requirement for vacancies in some occupational sectors by the employer; (v) compliance with local and industry-specific wage and working conditions by the employer. Furthermore, the employee must fulfil personal requirements, such as a university degree and several years of professional experience, but economic and social adaptability, language skills and age are also taken into account. In addition, they must have an apartment that meets their needs.

[562] The application must be submitted to the competent cantonal employment or migration authority. The authority carries out a preliminary examination. Applications are then forwarded to the State Secretariat for Migration (SEM) for approval. A visa is also required, which is issued by the cantonal migration authority.

[563] Non-EU citizens can be granted either a short-term residence permit, a residence permit or a cross-border commuter permit. An application for a permanent residence permit can be submitted after ten years of residence.

5.5.3 Taxation and Social Security

[564] Foreign employees are subject to *Swiss WHT*. The WHT obligation ends with the acquisition of a permanent residence permit.

[565] Under the system of WHT, the *employer is obliged* to deduct the income tax of its foreign employees directly from their wage payments and transfer it to the tax authorities. The taxes are owed either at the place of residence or at the place of work of the employees; the tax rates vary from canton to canton.

[566] If the annual income exceeds CHF 120 000, a regular tax return must be submitted. The tax is assessed on the basis of this return. The WHT already paid by the employer is deducted from the assessed tax liability. Any difference must be paid additionally or is refunded.

[567] Foreign employees must register with a *Swiss health insurance* company within three months of arrival or commencement of employment. If more than eight hours are worked per week, the employer pays the premiums for the accident insurance. Contributions to *old-age, survivors' and disability insurance* are compulsory. They are deducted directly from the salary. The contribution is 10.60% of the salary (as of 1 January 2020), half of which is paid by the employer (*see* paragraph [550]). Insurance with a pension fund is compulsory for employees with a certain income or above. Self-employed persons can voluntarily join a pension fund.

[568] Within the scope of the AFMP with the EU, the following regulations mu also be considered: by adoption of an EU regulation into Swiss law in 201 employees are subject to the *social security* obligation of the country of employme if they work there for more than 25% of the week. This is particularly relevant f cross-border commuters. In addition, insignificant activities (up to 5% of workir time or income) are not taken into account when assigning the social security ob gation. Management of a company (e.g., an activity on the board of directors) never considered insignificant.

5.5.4 Restrictions on Foreign Managers and Directors

[569] Until 2008, the majority of the members of the board of directors of a cor pany had to reside in Switzerland and hold Swiss citizenship. After the deletion this regulation, neither a residence nor a nationality requirement applies. Ho ever, the company must be represented by at least one person who is *resident in Sw zerland*. This person must be either a member of the board of directors or manager appointed by the board.

[570] Foreign directors from the EU without residence in Switzerland must repo to the relevant authority if their activity exceeds eight calendar days per year.

5.5.5 Liability

[571] Swiss law stipulates the *personal liability of directors and managing directors*. Th so-called directors' and officers' liability presupposes financial loss, which must causal to a breach of duty under company law. Finally, there must be personal fau on the part of the executive body. The liability covers not only board members b all persons in a company who have a decisive influence on the decision-making (s called factual organs).

[572] The liability risk can be minimised by strictly complying with company la and, in particular, by strictly avoiding any mixing of business and private asse Furthermore, the board of directors may delegate the management of a compa that does not concern its core competencies to individual members of the board third parties (officers). However, this means that the board of directors can on release itself from liability if it complies with its duties regarding the careful sele tion, instruction and supervision of management. In particular, the superviso duty includes extensive duties of intervention towards the management. In adc tion, the *business-judgment-rule* also offers a certain degree of protection: decisio that have been made on the basis of appropriate information and are free of co flicts of interest are only reviewed by the courts with restraint. Discharge decisio also offer a form of protection.

[573] Nevertheless, it is advisable to have sufficient insurance cover. So-call D&O insurance (directors' and officers' liability) usually covers the following: defence against unjustified claims (duty to defend); (ii) compensation for financ loss resulting from actions and omissions in breach of duty; (iii) assumption of leg costs and all other agreed costs.

6 ACCOUNTING TREATMENT

(by Cédric Jenoure, Sascha Wohlgemuth)

6.1 The General Accounting Framework

[574] Accounting rules differ in Switzerland according to whether companies are incorporated or not. In fact, only *incorporated companies* are required to observe specific accounting guidelines. The accounting requirements are less stringent for other companies and for traders entered as individuals in the Commercial Register. All companies are nevertheless advised to prepare annual accounts as they provide a comprehensive overview of the financial position of the company and give the company director a powerful tool for managing the company. The company will be required to present its accounts to banks when it applies for a loan.

[575] Moreover, accounting is one of the areas in which the Swiss concept of commercial confidentiality is particularly significant: only *listed* companies and companies that have outstanding bonds are required to publish their accounts.

6.1.1 Obligations Arising from Entry in the Commercial Register

[576] Under the Code of Obligations, if entry in the Commercial Register is obligatory, accounting is as well and the company should keep the books that are required by the type and extent of [its] business. These books must show the company's financial position, its position in terms of debts and receivables relating to its operations and the annual financial results.

[577] Companies that are entered in the *Commercial Register* must accordingly keep accounts, draw up a statement of stock and prepare a balance sheet and a profit and loss account at the end of each financial year. However, there is no legal requirement that specifies the presentation of accounts, the type of accounting or a chart of accounts to be adopted by the company, except for limited companies.

6.1.2 Principles Relating to the Balance Sheet and the Profit and Loss Account

[578] *Article 957a CO* nevertheless specifies the general principles to which the balance sheet and the profit and loss account are subject: '[...] they must be complete, clear and easy to consult, so that interested parties can inform themselves as precisely as possible of the company's financial situation'.

[579] The obligation to keep accounting records is accordingly imposed with the aim of facilitating and improving the management of companies.

[580] Moreover, it is noted that the concept of a *'true and fair view'* is not expressly stated as the purpose of preparing financial statements.

6.1.3 Consolidated Accounts

[581] Pursuant to Article 963a CO, the *parent company* of a corporate group i obliged to prepare consolidated accounts if the group attains two of the followin thresholds in two successive financial years:

- total assets of CHF20 m;
- sales of CHF40 m;
- 250 workers as an annual average.

6.1.4 Retention of Accounting Documents

[582] Regardless of the legal form of companies, the *original* accounting record must be retained for ten years at the registered office of the company (Article 958 CO). They must comprise:

- all the books or registers prepared by the company;
- all correspondence received and copies of correspondence sent.

[583] In the age of digitisation, the law no longer requires paper form. Accountin documents can be stored digitally, provided that they are consistent with the busi ness transactions and can be made readable again at any time.

6.2 Accounting Standards in Switzerland

[584] There are no *accounting standards* prescribed by law or the CO. Only genera principles must be observed by all companies that are required to keep accounts although limited companies have to comply with additional obligations. Neverthe less, Swiss GAAP FER standards for the presentation of accounts have been estab lished (*see* paragraphs [585] et seq.)

6.2.1 The 'Swiss GAAP FER' Standards

[585] The Swiss Association for Audit, Tax, and Fiduciary has appointed a commis sion to prepare *recommendations on the presentation of accounts*. The purpose of thi commission is to improve the comparability of annual accounts and the quality o information as well as to bring Swiss standards as closely in line as possible wit international standards on the presentation of accounts.

[586] Swiss GAAP FER constitute comprehensive recommendations on the pre sentation of accounts. The standards must be applied in their entirety. Matters tha are not addressed in these standards should be treated in accordance with genera principles.

[587] The adoption of these standards is not obligatory; they are solely intended t assist companies and to ensure that their accounts meet the requirements of th CO.

[588] These standards are recommendations; they are by no means as comprehensive as the US GAAP or IFRS standards.

6.2.2 Listed Companies

[589] The *'SIX' Swiss Exchange* based in Zurich decided with effect from 2005 that all the companies listed on the main market of the Swiss Exchange would be obliged to apply either the IFRS or US GAAP accounting standards.

[590] A new listing regulation came into force on °6 December 2021:dfr-en.pdf (ser -ag.com)

6.3 Accounting Obligations Imposed on Ltds

[591] *Ltds*, particularly if listed on a stock exchange, are subject to stricter rules. However, these rules apply to other types of companies, namely the LLCs, through references to provisions relating to these companies.

6.3.1 The Balance Sheet and the Profit and Loss Account

[592] The Act of 1 July 1992 on Ltds defines the 'generally accepted principles' specified in the CO in more detail. The balance sheet and profit and loss account must therefore comply with the following principles:

- *completeness* of the annual accounts;
- *clarity* and materiality of the information;
- *prudence*;
- assessment as a *going concern*;
- *consistency in presentation* and valuation;
- *prohibition of offsetting* assets and liabilities, or expenses and income.

6.3.2 Presentation of the Accounts

[593] The presentation of the profit and loss account and the balance sheet must comply with the very general model provided by the Act of 1 July 1992 (cf. paragraph [592]).

Minimum Structure of the Profit and Loss Account (or Appropriation Account)

Expenditure	Income
Materials and goods	Sales or fees
Personnel costs	

Financial expenses	Financial income
Amortisation/depreciation	Proceeds from sale of fixed assets
Non-operating expenses	Non-operating income
Non-recurring expenses	Non-recurring income

Minimal Structure of the Balance Sheet

Assets	Liabilities
Current assets	Debt capital
Cash	
Receivables from sales or provision of services	Debt from sales or provision of services
	Other short-term debts
Other receivables	Long-term debts
Stocks	Provisions for risks and charges
Fixed assets	Equity
Financial fixed assets	
Tangible fixed assets	Share capital
Intangible fixed assets	Capital by participation
	Legal reserve
	Other reserves
	Profit or loss

[594] In addition, the annual accounts must show the amounts for the precedin financial year.

[595] In order to improve the readability of annual accounts, Ltds are required t attach explanatory notes.

6.3.3 Publication of the Accounts

[596] Listed companies and companies that have outstanding bonds must publis their annual accounts and their consolidated financial statements together with th audit reports in the *Swiss Gazette of Commerce*. These documents are available for consultation for a period of one year.

[597] Creditors who have a legitimate interest may also consult the annual accounts.

6.3.4 Statutory Audit of Accounts

[598] The detailed statutory provisions on the audit of annual accounts are contained in the section on limited companies (Articles 727–731a CO). However, they apply to other types of companies by means of the references contained in the statutory provisions on these legal entities

[599] In fact, since 1 January 2008, a new Act on Ltds and the Licensing and Oversight of Auditors and its implementing ordinance established a new definition of the audit obligation that applies to all legal entities.

[600] The legal form of a legal entity is no longer a decisive factor in determining whether a legal entity must have an *auditor*: its size and economic importance that are the determining factors.

[601] The CO makes a distinction between the ordinary audit and the limited audit. SMEs that do not exceed certain size criteria may, under certain conditions, opt out of appointing an audit firm.

[602] In accordance with Article 727 CO, the following companies must have their accounts reviewed by an auditor in an ordinary audit:

(1) publicly traded companies; these are companies:
   - which have shares listed on a stock exchange;
   - which have bonds outstanding;
   - the assets or the turnover of which represent at least 20% of the consolidated accounts of a company that has shares listed on a stock exchange or has bonds outstanding;

(2) other companies that exceed two of the following thresholds in two successive financial years:
   - balance sheet total: CHF20 m;
   - sales revenue: CHF40 m;
   - 250 full-time employees as an annual average.

(3) companies that are required to prepare consolidated accounts.

[603] If the aforementioned conditions are not satisfied, the company must nevertheless arrange an ordinary audit when so required by shareholders or members who together represent 10% of the share capital. This option is also open to members who are personally liable or who are under an obligation to make additional financial contributions (cf. Article 818, paragraph 2 and Article 906, paragraph 2 CO).

[604] The ordinary audit of the annual accounts may also be stipulated in the articles of association or may be decided by the general meeting (opting up).

[605] A limited audit is required if the aforementioned conditions for the ordina audit are not satisfied. It is possible to opt out of the limited audit with the agre ment of all the shareholders or members and if the number of full-time staff do not exceed ten as an annual average.

[606] Associations (Articles 60-79 CC) must have an ordinary audit of their annu accounts when two of the following thresholds are exceeded in two successive fina cial years:

- balance sheet total: CHF10 m;
- sales revenue: CHF20 m;
- staff: fifty full-time positions as an annual average (Article 69b, paragraph CC).

[607] However, an association must have a *limited audit* of its accounts by an audit if so required by a member of the association who is personally liable or who under an obligation to make additional financial contributions (Article 69b, par graph 2 CC).

[608] Foundations that have exceeded two of the aforementioned thresholds two successive financial years are also required to obtain an ordinary audit (Artic 83b CC). This is subject to the application of specific legislation.

[609] Other foundations that do not attain the aforementioned thresholds mu obtain a limited audit of their accounts without the possibility of opting out, unle exempted by the supervisory authority (Article 83b, paragraph 2 CC). Foundatio with a balance sheet total that exceeds CHF200 000 cannot be exempted from th obligation to appoint an audit firm.

[610] Family foundations and ecclesiastical foundations are exempt from the ob gation to appoint an audit firm.

6.4 M&A Accounting

6.4.1 The Purchase Method

[611] For take-overs and acquisitions, the principal method of accounting is th *purchase method*. Results of the acquired company may be brought into the grou accounts from the beginning of the year in which the acquisition takes place, ar disposals eliminated from the beginning of the year in which the disposal is mad This may lead to a material distortion of trading performance. The statement assets and liabilities in the acquired company has to be done at their fair value the acquiring group. Hidden reserves necessitate major assets to be calculat separately. Differences resulting from this procedure in fair values of the assets ar liabilities and the return paid, qualifies as positive, or negative, goodwill.

[612] Accounting standards offer two possible treatments: (a) The first method current and allows carrying the *goodwill balance* as an asset in the balance sheet, ar amortise it over its economic life as an annual charge, through the P+L accour

The second method (b) was the long-time Swiss standard and implies an immediate write-off of the goodwill balance against reserves. This method eliminates goodwill against the share premium account.

[613] An instant write-off was considered to represent the value of a share after its acquisition. But for tax purposes, value adjustments and depreciations on prime costs under the Federal Act on Direct Tax can qualify as taxable profit, provided they are no longer justified (Article 62 paragraph 4 Federal Act on Direct Tax). An immediate write-off affects the fair value after an acquisition and qualifies as post-merger act.

6.4.2 Pooling-of-Interests Method

[614] According to the *pooling-of-interests method*, the carrying amount of the investment is offset against the proportionate balance sheet equity of the subsidiary. Any remaining asset (liability) difference must be offset against group reserves. Hidden reserves and, if applicable, goodwill are not uncovered, so that book value is continued here. In subsequent years, there are no negative effects on earnings due to amortisation of goodwill or write-downs on hidden reserves. Although there are restrictions on the use of this method under IFRS and US GAAP, this method is still allowed under Swiss law.

[615] This method applies often in share-for-share acquisitions.

6.4.3 Provisions

[616] A *provision* is a probable obligation based on an event in the past, the amount and/or maturity of which is uncertain but estimable. A provision has to be recognised if the following conditions are met cumulatively:

- event of the past that took place before the balance sheet date;
- leads to a present obligation (legal or factual);
- whose fulfilment is expected to be associated with a cash outflow, the amount of which is estimable.

[617] *Restructuring provisions* may only be those directly related to the restructuring expenses (e.g., severance payments, consulting services, tax implications). Expenses must be forcibly incurred and must not be related to the continuing activities of the target company. Not recoverable are therefore costs for the future business operation such as the retraining of further employees or investing in new systems or distribution networks. Basically, not resettable are compensation to remunerated employees (e.g., path compensation). Future operating losses are not allowed as restructuring provisions. However, the announcement or implementation of a restructuring measure can lead to dismantling costs for which a provision also has to be raised.

6.4.4 Purchase Price Determination

[618] The *acquisition cost or purchase price* of an acquisition includes the assets liabilities incurred or assumed by the buyer and issued equity instruments in exchange for obtaining control of the acquired company. Also to be added to the acquisition costs are ancillary costs which have become necessary to complete the transaction.

[619] In many cases, as part of a company acquisition, agreements are made that provide for subsequent performance by the acquiring company to the seller if clearly defined future events occur (earn out). These are usually made in the form of payments when a previously fixed amount such as Earnings Before Interest and Taxes (EBIT) or share price development is exceeded. These *conditional acquisition costs* (contingent considerations) have to be taken into account in the purchase price and recognised as a provision for miscellaneous items, provided that their occurrence is probable and their value can be reliably determined. Earn-out payments over several years are classified as short-term and long-term provisions. Within the first two years from the closing date, adjustments to earn-out provisions (due to reassessment of the provisioning requirement or due to a different pay-out) are recognised as a correction to the related goodwill. This prospectively changes the amortisation expense of goodwill over the remaining useful life. If, after two years from the closing date, adjustments to earn-out provisions or other disbursements have to be made, the difference in value will be captured in the income statement.

6.4.5 Purchase Price Allocation

[620] In the case of a *Purchase Price Allocation (PPA)*, the acquisition costs of the company acquisition are allocated to the individually acquired assets, liabilities and contingent liabilities measured at their fair value, and any goodwill or negative goodwill is determined.

[621] Under the PPA, there is usually a difference between the acquisition cost of a business combination (purchase price) and the acquired interest in the fair value of identifiable assets, liabilities and contingent liabilities. If the acquisition costs exceed the proportionate value of the net assets acquired, goodwill results, which is capitalised as an intangible asset at the time of acquisition and subsequently amortised on schedule. If the proportionate value of the acquired net assets is higher than the acquisition cost (lucky buy), this results in negative goodwill, which is reflected in the period result.

6.4.6 Intangible Assets

[622] When acquiring a company, it is necessary to examine which *intangible assets* have been acquired. Applying the recognition criteria for intangible assets may result in the recognition of assets that the acquired company had previously not capitalised as an asset.

[623] Assets to be regarded as fundamentally capitalisable:

- Registered trademarks and logos.
- Internet addresses (domains).
- Software as well as online shops.
- Rights of use (e.g., for water).
- Acquired customer relationships.

[624] Acquired customer relationships can be considered personal intangible assets and may therefore be written off within a maximum of five years. All intangible assets are subject to the principle that the recoverable amount is measured on the basis of a measurable future benefit within the framework of any necessary impairment test.

6.4.7 Treatment of Acquisition Costs

[625] Only those *costs* can be capitalised which arise out of the acquisition. The costs incurred in the preparation of a transaction, for example, due diligence or general legal and business advice, should not be capitalised. These should already be charged to the income statement on an ongoing basis and are not capitalised retroactively.

6.4.8 Retroactive Effect

[626] Under Swiss merger law, *retroactivity* of six months is allowed, provided that all necessary documents are submitted to the Commercial Register not later than 30 June of the current year (*see* circular letter no. 5, section 4.1.2.2.3, of the FTA). Hence, profits of an intra-yearly merged target company can be brought into the acquiring company's P+L account as of 1 January of the current year.

7 FUTURE DEVELOPMENTS

(by Elisa Aliotta)

7.1 The Modernisation of Swiss Company Law

[627] For the past decade, the Swiss Federal Council and Parliament have been working on the revision of Swiss legislation on Ltds with the aim of modernising Swiss company law. After a preliminary draft was put forward in 2014 and consultation proceedings were carried out, the Federal Council on 23 November 2016 presented its new draft bill for the company law reform along with the explanatory report (Dispatch) and submitted it to Parliament. On 19 June 2020, the draft bill was adopted by the Parliament.

[628] The revised draft bill aims to enhance the flexibility of the provisions of incorporation and capital structures as well as to modernise the requirements con cerning the annual general meetings of stock corporations. Further goals entail th strengthening of the rights of shareholders and gender equality for executives i listed companies and transparency regarding financial flows in the raw materia sector. The draft bill further incorporates numerous changes to 'traditional' corpc rate law to provide companies with more flexibility. Such changes include, *inter alic* the permissibility of share capital denominated in foreign currency and the intrc duction of a so-called capital band which will allow the board of directors to decid on capital increases and decreases within such band.

[629] The new law also modernises the provisions for the general meeting b introducing the possibility to exercise shareholders' rights electronically, for th general meeting to be held in writing and to be carried out virtually and by elec tronic methods. Furthermore, the new law introduces gender quotas for large liste companies that will become binding after a transitional period of five year According to such quota, each gender should be represented by at least 30% on th board of directors and 20% on executive management. Further changes include th introduction of transparency rules for major companies in the exploitation of natu ral resources industry aimed at fighting corruption and legal changes to lim excessive pay packages at large companies (tracing back to the so-called Minde initiative) currently regulated by the Swiss Ordinance against Excessive Compensa tion.

[630] After a few new regulations such as the gender quota for listed companie and transparency requirements for commodity companies already entered int force on 1 January 2022, the revised bill will take full effect at on 1 January 2023

7.2 Amendments to the Anti-Money Laundering Act

[631] On 26 June 2019, the Federal Council adopted the Dispatch on the amenc ment of the AMLA. The proposal reflects the main recommendations from th Financial Action Task Force's (FATF) mutual evaluation report on Switzerland. Th revised AMLA introduces due diligence obligations as well as a mandatory notifica tion reporting system of suspicious activities on advisors. The revised AMLA wa adopted by the Federal Parliament in March 2021 and is expected to enter int force by the middle of 2022.

7.3 The Responsible Business Initiative

[632] In April 2015, a coalition of Swiss civil society organisations launched a pul lic initiative to hold Swiss-based companies legally accountable if their oversea subsidiaries violate human rights or environmental standards (the Responsib Business Initiative). The Responsible Business Initiative seeks to implement th United Nations Guiding Principles on Business and Human Rights by introducin mandatory due diligence in respect of human rights and the environment. The initiative did not find approval in the corporate sector and was criticised for being too harsh and harmful to Swiss business interests.

[633] On 29 November 2020, the public initiative to hold Swiss-based companies legally accountable if their overseas subsidiaries violate human rights or environmental standards (the Responsible Business Initiative) was rejected at the ballot box. Instead, the counterproposal issued by the Parliament was adopted. The counterproposal obliges companies to report on human rights and environmental standards and to conduct due diligence with regard to child labour and mineral sourcing from conflict areas. The counterproposal does not include an additional liability provision as envisaged by the initiative.

[634] The Federal Council has enacted the new provisions in the Swiss Code of Obligations (CO) and the corresponding implementing provisions with effect from 1 January 2022. Switzerland thus has internationally coordinated legislation that is primarily based on the regulation currently in force in the European Union.

7.4 The Introduction of Investment Control Measures

[635] The Federal Parliament requested the Federal Council to consider the potential risks of state-backed companies from emerging economies increasingly investing in Switzerland and respective investment control measures to address such risks. The request from the Federal Parliament is the result of the increasing number of notable M&A transactions by Chinese firms in Switzerland and growing concerns that such direct investment in Switzerland may result in a loss of jobs and expertise.

[636] On 25 August 2021, the Federal Council defined the initial principles for controlling foreign investments via a planned draft bill for a Swiss investment control regime. The key principles presented by the Federal Council aim at protecting the public order and security against threats or endangerment entailed in acquisitions of Swiss companies by foreign investors and at preventing substantial distortions of competition by acquisitions of foreign state or state-related investors. The Federal Council proposed that a sector-specific review shall apply in the event of threats or endangerments to public order or security. In case of takeovers by states or state-related investors, the Federal Council proposes a sector-independent review.

[637] It is expected that the Federal Council's consultation draft bill will be submitted in summer 2022.

www.ingramcontent.com/pod-product-compliance
Ingram Content Group UK Ltd.
Pitfield, Milton Keynes, MK11 3LW, UK
UKHW020147290926
15471UKWH00004B/746

9 789403 543642